Endorsements

MW01141468

Making God Visible challenge Christians. Betty Alexander's narrative offers readers keys to what it means to truly and fully live in the Kingdom of Heaven.

—**Cornelia Becker Seigneur**
Speaker, Freelance Journalist
Author, *Writer Mom Tales*
and *Images of America*
West Linn, Oregon

Betty—It was truly a real joy to do a slow and methodical review of your new book, *Making God Visible.*

I've known Betty Alexander, her life and living testimony since 1995 as her professor at MHBC. Her first book opens her life to you through an insightful anointing and revelation of the Word of God.

If you are searching for God, this book will lead you to Him. If you are developing a deeper relationship with God, this book will allow you to find out where you are and challenge you to get where you want to be! Each chapter is a personal challenge that can lead you to personal victories in Christ. This book is about you and your God . . . . How well do you know Him? Accept the challenge. This book is a must read.

> Lack of heavenly glory nails our feet to the ground enslaving us to the world's reign. Our eyes see only the visible, and we are unable to soar to new highs with God. We are unable to see beyond ourselves.

Do you want to go places in the Spirit that you have never gone . . . . read this book. Betty Alexander will challenge you and lead you to "another place in God."

Making God Visible is chocked full of "life lessons" that are brought to life through Betty's revelation of the Word. God has used her to reveal His personhood through His word to her, and then she applies that revelation, of who He is, to practical answers to life's dilemmas.

Betty . . . . thanks for the honor and privilege . . .

—**Rev. Larry and Debbie Hrovat**
President & Founder of Faith of The Nations
International Missionary Evangelist
International Conference Speaker
Parker, Colorado

MAKING
GOD
VISIBLE

MAKING
GOD
VISIBLE

I know Jesus,
I recognize Paul,
BUT WHO ARE YOU?

Betty Alexander

REDEMPTION
PRESS

Published by Redemption Press, PO Box 427, Enumclaw, WA 98022.

ISBN 13: 978-1-63232-511-2 (Print)
        978-1-63232-512-9 (ePub)
        978-1-63232-513-6 (Mobi)

Library of Congress Catalog Card Number: 2010911213

DEDICATION

To all believers who, like Elisha, dream of more in the Kingdom of Heaven and to those who desire more of the Holy Spirit while they are seeking to take the next step with Jesus to do exploits right now on the earth. To the hungry hearts that struggle to taste and perceive the unique purpose and mission that Father God has designed for them.

ACKNOWLEDGMENTS

FIRST, I WANT to acknowledge my parents, Dalbert and Jean Alexander, whose actions and words were always encouraging, saying that, "You can do anything that you put your mind to," and "Never give up." They demonstrated that if we are willing to take a step forward, there is always a way. They were always there, dependable, loving, and extremely giving to all. Thanks especially to Mom, who after accepting Jesus always took us to church. I am grateful to both of my parents, who set good standards for us.

The encouragement especially from my sister Liz, who told me of places where God is visiting in Revival and His heroes in this time. We (Liz and her husband, Steve, with granddaughter Alyssa) went to the Brownsville's Revival and other places where the bold and courageous ministered.

To Valerie, my sister in the Lord, an Intercessor, who continued to push me to finish this book. And to Tatyana, a true witness for Jesus, whose miracle to me assured me of God's answer to publish this book at such a time as this. For the knowledge gained from pastors, professors, friends, and family.

Now, because of our unity in the knowledge and love of the Lord and her insights and suggestions of words that were invaluable in the preparation of this book, my special appreciation goes to my longtime sister in the Lord, Dana Canary, music minister, singer, and prayer warrior. Without her help, this book would not have been possible. I am grateful for her endurance in reviewing the manuscript's many rewrites and for her encouragement, saying, "Just look at what we're learning." Because of her dedication and joy in the Lord, she is chief among those whom I want to acknowledge.

Thank you all for being led by the Holy Spirit. Thank you, Holy Spirit, for revealing dark saying, mysteries of the Lord, and the Helper in my serving Jesus.

Deuteronomy 29:29

CONTENTS

PREFACE

ALL MY LIFE I have wondered why I could not do the things Jesus said Christians would be doing. Having believed in Jesus from early childhood, I noticed that my life lacked the signs and wonders found in the Bible.

This book tells of my journey and the journey of others as we pursue Heaven. It will inspire and encourage you with present-day events. Some of these events you may never have heard of, but they are life-giving and will stoke the fire of faith within you.

I have met many Christians who have no idea how to take steps toward living a fuller Christian life. I have been on prayer lines that are flooded with people with needs. Great burdens weigh our brothers and sisters down, yet few have found relief or help in the church. Therefore, some choose to go to what is in the world because they have not acquired intimacy with God nor do they know His remedies.

This book gives a view of living in the Kingdom of God. Within the pages of this book are ways to start breaking loose from a nominal Christian lifestyle. It only takes small beginnings to start to change and to affect the world for Jesus Christ. By giving you simple acts and key elements to focus on, this book will help you recognize the things God desires you to do.

This book will also share stories of some recognized Believers—those who have dared to believe and soared to new heights—have accomplished great things and thereby have made God visible to others.

But, we must first learn God's truth from Holy Scripture. Then we can learn from those in the past and those in the present who have joined the ranks of the heroes of God.

By defining terms and showing some examples of unseen strongholds, Believers can be free to live big for God. A new slant on truth can transform minds and rouse God's people to dig deeper, love harder, and live stronger. Readers will see questions at the end of the chapters to contemplate; my hopes are that they will inspire you to be bold and courageous.

HELP FOR THE READER

Capitalizing all nouns and pronouns concerning God and His Kingdom, wherever found in this text, will place Him in the place of superiority. There will be no capitals regarding the enemy unless starting a sentence. By doing so, my hope is to stimulate the reader to remember that words of the world are weak compared to those of God. By capitalizing Believers and Saints, we are reminded that we are made in the image of God.

In addition, all Scripture references numbered (i.e.#2871) within this book are from: *The New Strong's Exhaustive Concordance of the Bible*; and hereafter referred to as *Strong's*; references for the Hebrew and Greek will be from *Young's* and refers to *Young's Concise Critical Bible Commentary*; *Hebrew* refers to *Gesenius' Hebrew and Chaldee Lexicon*; *Greek* refers to *The Complete Word Study Dictionary*; IGENT refers to *The Interlinear Greek-English New Testament*; CJB refers to *The Complete Jewish Bible*; *Smith's* refers to *William Smith's Bible Dictionary, 1948*; *Webster's* refers to *Merriam-Webster's Reference Library, 1994*.

May you get a view of the Kingdom of Heaven and be challenged to live a full life for Christ as you read this book.

—Betty Alexander

Chapter 1

RECOGNIZED AS CHRISTIANS

HOW DO OTHERS see us when they do not acknowledge us as Christians? Even though we live in the world, we are not to be like the people in it. The difference between us and non-believers, who live carnal lives, should be easy to discern. If the world recognizes us as common people with carnal/sensual traits, we become acceptable to them. However, Believers have distinct characteristics that make us uncommon and set us apart from the world while making us known and loved by God. The quality that makes Christians different is that we esteem one Holy God of truth and power and serve only Him, while people who are worldly serve multiple vain idols. Because of the importance of identification, when we lack the characteristics that identify us as the followers of Jesus, we miss the elements that validate us as Believers.

Jesus promised that if one has faith in Him, that person would do more than Jesus did because He went to the Father and has sent us the empowerment of the Spirit of Truth (see John 14:12–17). He added that if the world hated Him, it would hate us also (see Matt. 10:22; 24:9; Mark 13:13; John 15:18). Christians are hated because they will not let non-believers enjoy and conduct life in sin, but will confront them with the need to change to a life that is complete in Christ.

The earth shook when Jesus came and changed the world for all time. Not as an earthquake but a supernatural shaking took place in the lives of people (see Matt. 16:24–26). Humans never like change, especially not change that involves giving up the power and control they think they possess. However, there is a power that God gives humankind that surpasses all the power and control in the natural and the elements. People who had this power displayed exploits, doing extraordinary things for God throughout the ages. They are the remnant of God.

EARLY CHRISTIANS

Something was different about the early Christians. They were people of power and of love who endured all things. They didn't need to go around confessing to be followers of Jesus, because even non-believers knew them and pointed fingers at them, declaring, "See, there's a Christian."

During the years after the resurrection, people recognized and feared the early Christians who willingly laid down their lives for Jesus.

Christians were different because of their love of bringing humankind to Jesus and because of their desire to increase the Kingdom of God on earth. They were lovers of God who could not remain quiet. They knew humankind resided in darkness on a destructive path to hell, but that Light had come to deliver them.

THE PROPHETS OF OLD

The prophets of old, like the early Christians, were feared and gained respect because of their relationship with the God of Truth. Fearful non-believers persecuted and hated them, even putting them to death. The prophets possessed a frightening aura. When they came to town, often traveling many miles to deliver a message to the people from God, the townspeople were fearful. Having been in Israel, I can picture the scenario: From the guard's tower high above the wall encasing the town, the watchman would see the prophet approaching, riding on his mule or walking on the well-traveled road toward the town gates. The sentinel would alert the officials by sending a messenger running to notify them. A respected official would come out of his place of security to meet with the approaching man of God. Trembling, the whole township would wonder, "Is he coming to bring peace or not? Will God's Prophet bring the word from God as a blessing or a curse?" Timidly, and with a humble attitude, the official would meet the prophet outside the city gates and respectfully ask, "Have you come for the prosperity or destruction of this place?"

God's chosen often wore a mantle, perhaps of varied colors. "Mantle" rendered in *Smith's* means: a coat, cloak, or robe. It goes on to say, "Elijah the prophet probably wore a mantle of sheepskin" (pages 379, 380 paraphrased). It was woolly and hence gave the prophet a look that was frightening. Prophets not only wore a mantle of natural hairy material, but also an unseen supernatural garment.

These men or women of God may have been found in king's palaces or living in remote areas. They won their battles against all odds. They closed the mouths of lions, had visions of the Kingdom of God, and they interpreted dreams that told of kingdoms through the ages. They survived the fire of a furnace seven times hotter than normal—it was so hot, it slew the strongest men who came to throw them into the blazing furnace (see Dan. 3:19–23). God's prophets called fire from Heaven to destroy soldiers and false prophets. They caused iron to float to the top of a river. They raised the dead, multiplied food, and prayed for rain to stop famine. Once, even bears came and ate the people who berated a prophet.

Like the lowing of cattle, these prophets called to the people of God to return and live out His commandments and ordinances. They were anointed with supernatural strength, outran chariots, and pulled down buildings. Miraculously, birds fed them, and they survived inside arks, whales, and heathen countries. These Believers' actions and words made them known to others. The hand of God was on them, and they carried God's Word in real time. In addition, as the writer in Hebrews 11:32–38 states, that time would fail to permit the telling of the heroes of God, Believers of whom the world was not worthy.

These acts continued into the lives of the first-century Christians as the power of the Holy Spirit was poured out on all Believers (see Joel 2:28, manifested in Acts 2:17). This prophecy, never rescinded, remains in full force today.

Today, God's heroes, as in the days of the Apostles, are recognized as having been with Jesus, not only because their views sound like those of Jesus, but because they are infused with firepower and the baptism of the Holy Spirit for witnessing. The Holy Spirit accompanied them, providing the miraculous. These Christians desired recognition by humankind for God's glory, not for self-glorification. Now, as then, bold Believers go everywhere preaching the good news of forgiveness through the blood of Jesus and making it known that the Kingdom of God has come near to them.

THE DISCIPLES

While in Greece at Antioch, disciples preached with signs following to non-believing Jews and the heathen Greeks, bringing many to Jesus. Here, something unthinkable happened. Disciples in "The Way" acquired a new name in Greek: *Christian* (see Acts 11:26). It would become permanent as down through the ages the name stuck. God's people no longer were called "The Way," but as foretold in Isaiah, the prophecy of a new name was fulfilled:

> The nations will see your righteousness, and all kings your glory; and you will be called by a new name which the mouth of the LORD will designate.
>
> —Isaiah 62:2 NASB

Because the nations (non-believers) recognize the anointing that the followers of Jesus Christ possess, they are now marked as Christians.

In the Greek, the word Christian comes "from the word for *anointed, that is the Hebrew name, Messiah,* the epithet of Jesus. Anointed is from the idea of *contact*; to smear or rub with oil, implying to be consecrated to an office or religious service: which means to *fear,* to go trembling in one's service. The purest essence of the word anointed means to *furnish what is needed!*"

"Christian" is a powerful word. Although humankind may use it disparagingly when viewing Jesus the Christ and His followers, with God it is highly esteemed and holds renown.

THE APOSTLES

Many people gained reverence for the Apostles when the sick were healed as Peter passed and his shadow fell on them (see Acts 5:15); handkerchiefs and aprons from Paul's body were carried to the sick and they recovered (see Acts 19:12); Apostles were translated; the dead were raised; demons were cast out; and the gospel was preached with great fervor. All of them had integrity. This code was tested at a meeting with the Apostles. When Ananias and Sapphira lied to the Holy Spirit and died (see Acts 5:1–10), news of this event spread throughout the community of Believers. Terror followed and none wanted to join the Apostles' rank, even though the Apostles were highly regarded. Nevertheless, even with the report of this event, people daily joined the Church as they believed on the Lord Jesus Christ (see Acts 5:14).

Early Christians, consecrated to their office, possessed the Kingdom, or perhaps a better statement would be the Kingdom possessed them. Their task was to bring humankind to the door of the Kingdom of Heaven, letting them know they were welcome to enter, if they chose to do so. Christians used every opportunity to share hope with the world's lost and hurting.

FORERUNNERS OF TODAY

In these last days, we have heard of a few Believers who have had signs and wonders accredited to them. Names such as Smith Wigglesworth, John G. Lake, Aimee Semple McPherson, and Kathryn Kuhlman are among those whose ministries were accompanied by mighty miracles. The sick were healed, the dead were raised, and demons were cast out.

Today, jails open and people such as Brother Andrew walk out, hidden from the view of those who would kill him for carrying the good news to the lost in the world. Mother Teresa's Missionaries of Charity feed thousands daily, turning none away. Billy Graham has brought millions to Jesus. In Europe, Graham is known as God's Gatling gun because his words so thoroughly hit the mark, striking hearts to repent, they lay aside their old life, and follow Jesus. Reinhard Bonnke and now Benny Hinn have had one million people accept Jesus Christ in one service!

Today, others such as David Hogan (Freedom Ministries) and Rolland and Heidi Baker (Iris Ministries) daily lay their lives down for the Kingdom of Heaven. Their affections are set on Christ. They press those living in darkness to come into the saving light of Jesus. The Holy Spirit is with them, confirming their words with signs following (see Mark 16:20). Every kind of healing occurs in their ministry such as blind eyes opened, deaf ears hearing, and leprosy cleansed. Other signs include: food multiplied and entire towns won to Jesus. These bold courageous people are among us today.

In addition, there are those of lesser note who love and live for Jesus—those who hungrily go after Jesus Christ and the Kingdom of God. Others, who live by the standards of the world, persecute and hate all of these people.

In Matthew 10:7–8 (CJB), Jesus said to His disciples, "As you go, proclaim, 'The Kingdom of Heaven is near,' heal the sick, raise the dead, cleanse those afflicted with *tzara'at* [skin diseases], expel demons. You have received without paying, so give without asking payment." This is a remarkable charge and one of extraordinary wonder beyond human capacity to understand. It is a commission taken seriously by those chosen of God.

With the preaching of the good news, many accept and enter into salvation. Others refuse to believe. Mark 16:16 says, "Whoever believes and is baptized will be saved, but whoever does not believe will be condemned."

A Unique People

Wherever Christians went, miracles, wonders, and signs followed them (see Acts 2:22, 43; 4:30; 5:12; Rom. 15:19; Heb. 2:4). In 2 Corinthians 12:12, they are marked by what the Holy Spirit did through their lives. The first Christians were known by their love for all humankind and for one another and for being fruitful. Christians were recognized by the fruit they produced: the fruit of their souls and the light that "consists in all goodness, righteousness and truth" (Eph. 5:9); "The fruit of the Spirit" (Gal. 5:22); and the fruit of their lips that confessed God's name (see Heb. 13:15). Today, this is what sets Believers apart as lovers of Jesus. They are marked as God's unique people.

Christians are different from worldly people. What makes a person unique? As I meditated on God's Word, I recognized common areas in my life that had to do with the condition of my heart and my lack of humble character. This made me a shortsighted lover of Christ, missing uncommon traits and not fully knowing that I was a pilgrim on the earth. I was not looking for a better country. In addition, I did not recognize that my inheritance was hidden in Christ. In my wrestling with God to come into the number of those recognized, I would have to die to my self-life. Even so, I am determined to change, just as others do who walk closely with God and see life from another Kingdom.

- How have I presented life in Christ to others?
- How have my actions and words sounded like Jesus'?
- As a unique person, what fruits are produced in my life?

Chapter 2

LIFE'S LOT

WE ARE ALL the children of God by faith in Christ Jesus, the seed of Abraham. We are heirs to the promise (see Gal. 3:27–29). Jesus died for our portion, making us joint-heirs with Him as adoptive sons (see Gal. 4:5; Rom. 8:17), and making us entitled to the possession of property, rank, title, and office of heir-ship (see Heb. 9:15–17). As the eldest son, Jesus received a double portion (see Deut. 21:17, *Smith's* page 194), and He willingly shares it with us *as we walk with Him*. By doing the business of Heaven, we start to occupy and possess the earth right now. Since we were born naked, we can take nothing out of this world when we die. Everyone will be rewarded according to their actions and desires in this lifetime (2 Cor. 5:10), for where their treasure is, there will their heart be also (see Matt. 6:21). The goals a person strives for designate their inheritance now and at the end of life. If we examine our objectives, we can see which of them relate to this earthly life and which goals help us store up treasures in Heaven for eternity. The mighty ones of God know the truth of sowing and reaping on earth, and they live with nothing holding them to this world.

FUTURE INHERITANCE

Our desires pull us in diverse directions, and they control our fate here and into the future. God's promises give us glimpses of our eternal destiny. However, the view of the full treasure is hidden from our sight. We see this depicted in the stories of various lives of the faithful in Hebrews 11 in the Bible. None of these Saints lived to see the full scope of their inheritance because it continued to play out on earth after they died. Their rewards are supernaturally stored in Heaven until time is no more. Such is the case seen in the life of Abraham whose inheritance extends into eternity. Supernaturally, he became the father of nations by his righteousness, faithfulness, and friendship with God. All sons of God have these three key elements established in their lives.

Abraham, by faith, became the father of one son, Isaac (see Gen. 22:2, 12, 16) whose line produced the Messiah. Isaac, the son conceived supernaturally, lived in the Promised Land and represented the covenant of laughter down through the ages. From Isaac came twins, Jacob and Esau, whom he blesses concerning things to come. One twin, Esau, is favored by humankind, and the other twin, Jacob, was favored by God. Jacob sees the doorway and ladder to Heaven, but goes his own way until the day of his wrestling with God. He then returns to live at Bethel (House of God). Jacob is the father of twelve sons, whose names are on the gates of Heaven.

Joseph, trained to oversee the family business, is the favored son of this father, Jacob. God's plan was that Joseph would run an empire to provide and protect the chosen people of God. Before he dies, Jacob blesses both the sons of Joseph, who are half Hebrew, and half Egyptian. Knowing God's faithfulness, Joseph prophesies the departure of the Israelites from Egypt and commands that they bury his bones in the land of promise.

Moses, as a babe, escapes death in a basket (ark). He is raised as royalty. Later, because he sees the invisible God, he esteems the reproach of Christ greater riches than the treasures of Egypt. Looking ahead to his reward (see Heb. 11:26), Moses delivers the Hebrews from Egyptian bondage, is the presenter of God's law, and is called a friend of God.

In the New Testament, Paul, a Pharisee of Pharisees, kills Believers in "The Way" and later preaches this same gospel of grace to the Gentiles. For this he suffers persecution and is later killed. But, before his death, he writes a large portion of the New Testament showing generations to come how to live and die predestined by God. There is always a bigger and grander portion, for the God of Heaven gives promises that play out far beyond our dreams and physical lifetime.

Even so, life's fate holds our immediate attention, locked in our small view of our present circumstances. Our natural sight is limited to earth's sphere. Until we accept Jesus, we cannot see a better destiny. Yet, some are not living in that light as fully as they should/could. Jesus gives us the power to soar above the atmosphere of the earth and to be able to fly to new heights as we become sons of God.

The Apostles referred to Believers as "Saints," meaning, "not of the earth." As stated in Acts 26:18 (*Young's*), [To open their eyes and to turn] "*lit. 'turn (them) over from darkness* [to light and from the] *authority of the Adversary upon God, for their receiving forgiveness (lit. a sending away) of sins, and a lot among those sanctified (lit. set apart or declared not of the earth), by faith that is toward me.*" For Believers this is quite a powerful description for sojourners here on earth. Now, as Saints, we are no longer professional sinners—sin's slaves—living only to sin and missing the goal of the high calling that God has for us. Now we can attain the impossible as we strive to live in purity and holiness. We live as if from another country. We act as ambassadors ruled by that country's King—Jesus. It is He who calls us to move toward nobility. Before, we were casualties of war, but now, we fight a battle where our victory is certain. We fight a battle in our mind, home, work, country, and world. With the Kingdom's unlimited possibilities, our vision and plans are no longer confined to what we physically see but can be carried away into other realms with the promises of "the God who gives life to the dead, and calls things that are not as though they were" (see Rom. 4:17) for our inheritance. We are no longer confined, but are liberated to fight a war in the supernatural that enables us to make effective changes in the natural.

The valiant persistently pursues another country where tears are wiped away, where light and freedom exist, and where there is peace and joy. Knowing the quality of life that darkness has stolen from humankind, the fearless charge into the battle with the power of the blood of Jesus. The cry of His name is on their lips. With hearts full of compassion, they reach out to the wounded who are held captive by the adversary, for they see and love them as Jesus does.

PREDESTINED FOR REBIRTH

No human has ever taken God by surprise; no matter what the circumstances of a person's birth, no one has been born by accident. Born at a certain time and in a certain place, each person has been predestined to be adopted sons through Jesus Christ (see Eph. 1:5). They are predestined to be glorious, but they will not obtain glory until they are reborn. When a person experiences the new birth, his inherited worldly characteristics will not rule him as he continues turning toward God. Whether rich, poor, tall, or short, all are given the right to inherit a life that has been purchased by Jesus. He came that we "may have life, and have it to the full" (John 10:10). The Scriptures say that Abraham,

Job, and David died full of years. They had accomplished everything God had for them to do! Their indestructible inheritance lives on throughout the ages. This is amazing, especially considering all the things that they did wrong. These imperfect men fulfilled the destinies God planned for them. It is possible for each of us to have that said about our lives. Because they obtained it, we can too. They are our examples, cheering us on to the goal—the goal of having a life that is a witness to God's glory. We cannot comprehend God's plan and purpose for our lives all at once because His plan is too high for us. The Holy Spirit will reveal it a little at a time. Yielding to God's call, we grow to maturity, avoiding stretch marks and spiritual growing pains. He molds and shapes us into royalty.

Two Destinies

God's Word reveals examples of divine destiny. Here is one with two courses of inheritance: the story of Esau and Jacob, who are twins, but because of events in life that marred and extended them to their limits, each took a different path. Reflections of these events may remind us of our own lives. Both are called to be part of God's family. The two of them mature in the same culture. Their mother, Rebekah, loves Jacob, the homebody. Their father, Isaac, loves Esau, the hunter (see Gen. 25:27–28). Esau is the firstborn, and as such sees no need to guard his inheritance or his father's blessing. His vision is confined to the moment in which he lives. Jacob, however, is influenced by his mother and takes any opportunity he can to get ahead. He looks to the future. You may remember that this greedy nature is an inherited trait of Rebekah's who comes from a manipulative family. It is seen in the deceitful act she has Jacob do. She comes from the same family as Abraham, father of Isaac. We get a glimpse of the family character in the events that happen in Genesis 24 where Abraham's chief servant goes to a well at Nahor in polytheistic Mesopotamia. There, he offers a prayer for God to bring him Isaac's wife (see Gen. 24:12).

Rebekah saw the camels coming. It wasn't a strange sight; these ships of the desert are many and are heavy-laden. There must be treasures coming her way; all travelers have wares to trade. This man must be a master of many and a possessor of great wealth to have a caravan with men in attendance; all of them well dressed. The leader, a ramrod of a figure, looks elegantly clad as he sits on the top of the lead animal—what a grand beast it is. He sits in a saddle arrayed with the ornaments of the rich and a colorful plush fringe-edged saddle blanket, each corner adorned with a dangling knot. Everything so colorful. Humm, this is a wealthy man, indeed.

Rebekah is at the age to marry, and is always on the alert to attract the eye of a man of position! She has no desire to be the wife of a nobody and live in a small shanty doing hard toil all her life. No, her family has taught her well. She will not be one of those wives who marry for love. She'll choose position and wealth.

The caravans often arrive about the time when women come to draw water for their family at the well (see Gen. 24:11). Rebekah thinks in her heart that this caravan has traveled a long way. She has never seen them in Nahor before. All the merchants travel this main road through the country. They stop here to rest and water themselves, their animals, and of course to trade their wares. So while it's usual for a caravan to stop, this is certainly a prestigious group. Whoever the owner is, he and the chief servant will be putty in her hand! She is a young woman, the type men want to impress. When the opportunity comes, she'll be the first there and do whatever it takes to gain the best gifts.

As the dust settles from the tramping of the feet of men and beasts, all look hungry, and she knows they are thirsty from their trek across a dry wilderness. Rebekah, when asked, offers water to the leader, and to seal the luck-of-fortune, she offers to water the camels too! Later, Rebekah's family invites Abraham's servant in. He tells of his quest and displays the treasures for the price of a bride. They see that it is to their advantage to seize this opportunity, while not appearing to be overly eager to accept the offer. After all, what broker wants a relative who is a gold digger? Why not go for the fathers blessing for the first son (Isaac) and keep the ancestors' inheritance. Keeping this transaction in the family, they all can share the wealth. The deal is mutually settled, and Rebekah leaves for the land of plenty—her eyes fixed on position and wealth.

Later, as a mother who trains up her children, she tries to instill her family values in her two sons. Esau, the hunter, likes the freedom of being away from her apron strings and is eager to do things his way—sort of like the prodigal son. However, Jacob is content to remain close to his mother at home. He listens and understands the tricks of her family values.

Yahweh was not Jacob's God at this time but was the God of his father Isaac. With Rebekah's leading, Jacob went after the inheritance and the blessing. Through trickery and fraud, Jacob took what belonged to his older brother. Like his mother, Jacob did whatever it took to gain the best gifts. Life, as they knew it, fell apart when this act of treachery separated the family. Jacob fled for his life. This was not God's plan, but it showed passion on Jacob's part. After Jacob took a detour in his life, God turned his (Jacob's) wicked ways into a benefit. God set him up to come to the end of himself. Esau still prospered even though he did not care enough to guard his birthright and blessing. He took for granted the security of his birthright, and he let his fleshly appetites control him. Now, in second position as inheritor, Esau went his own way. Even though Esau never again gains renown with God, his lineage still fares well in the world. Jacob's line, though imperfect, continues to be immortalized.

We have a part to play as heirs of God. While it is true that He can handle anything, God desires to work with frail humans. God uses people who listen to Him and do His will. Those who are heroes with God have passion; they see further in life than just the moment. They know that there are rights of birth (new birth) and that the blessings of the Father are theirs. The Father in Heaven, who is a covenant God, has thoroughly set down what He will do if we will do what is right and just before Him. We dare not think that all is secure or believe we can reach our goal by being lazy or uninterested. Saints have a supernatural God who has given them a supernatural life to live right now. With passion, we rouse ourselves to go after what God has set aside for us.

By the way, do not expect worldly people to do what God wants—why would they? They are not of His household. They are strangers who do not have their lot in the land of the living as we do. They are the walking dead, and their inheritance is in the land of constant burning. We have eternal hope. There is always an inheritance, whether we are of the Kingdom of God or the kingdom of the adversary. The wrath of God is coming upon the worldly (see Col. 3:6). However, those who are recognized by God know where their inheritance is, and they are busy storing up treasures where moth and rust won't destroy, and thieves do not break in to steal (see Matt. 6:20; Luke 12:33). They are busy doing the Heavenly Father's business here on earth, often with unperceived powers.

- What things have I been storing in Heaven?
- As a Saint, *not of this earth*, called to nobility, how have I seen beyond the moment?
- How have I guarded my divine destiny?

Chapter 3

THE FATHER'S BUSINESS

SINCE OUR HEAVENLY Father is eager to give us the Kingdom, why do so few people manifest the Kingdom in their lives? We have not grasped that something is missing. Because there is a criterion, we must seek the Kingdom of Heaven! When faced with this type of mandate preceding such a gift, Believers are faced with a choice to make: ignore what Holy Scripture says or embrace the humbling of the Lord and say "no" to self and seek righteousness and the Kingdom of God first. *Then* all things will be added (see Matt. 6:33). To inherit the Kingdom and its treasured mysteries, we must be willing to turn to wisdom not acquired by human intelligence and achievement. Making a decision to hunt for the secrets of the heavenly Kingdom (see Matt. 13:44) should be our first and primary focus. Even though the process will be crushing, it is also cleansing as God makes contrite our obstinate nature. As the hardness of our heart is transformed into power [as talc rock was crushed into powered talc], we come into alignment with the truth and justice of the Father in Heaven; we become pliable in humility. God resists the proud. Those who are self-reliant will only produce wind—their labors are in vain (see Jude vv. 11–13).

VIEWS OF HEAVEN

The Bible gives us a view of the way the Kingdom of Heaven operates. By telling parables, Jesus related stories so the uninterested would *not get his meaning*. But to the interested—his followers—he spoke plainly (see Luke 8:9–10). He gave us a view into the supreme rule of Heaven.

He compared things on earth to those in another country (Heaven) so Believers could grasp God's Kingdom and understand the true way to live.

Some people have made the connection with the unseen realm and have lived it out. One such person was Pope John Paul II. While watching a special on his life, I was impressed regarding his great zeal for God's will. In Poland, he was an unassuming priest who ended up changing the nation because of his love for God. The Polish people said that he gave them back their identity, and in so doing, gave them tools with which to fight. Solidarity was a silent movement that was very forceful in Poland. A Polish person said that once you enjoy freedom, it changes your entire behavior. The Pope often said to the people, "Be not afraid," as he demonstrated passive action. He typified certain characteristics that were like Jesus. As the Pope brought the eyes of the world back to moral conduct, he also took a hard stand on elevating only Jesus to the place of worship. Pope John Paul II influenced the world for good.

TOOLS OF IDENTITY

As a man, Jesus was not someone humankind noticed. Nevertheless, the world was changed and continues to change even today because of His life. Jesus always tells us to "fear not." He gives us tools of identity, a good mind, and boldness with which to fight and to become more than conquerors by His name. His occupation on earth revealed the enterprise to be lived by every Believer. Our renewed behaviors change our stance to live as Jesus lived.

BUSINESS

One day, while walking through the living room, I heard the words, "Be about the Father's business," spoken loudly, it seemed aloud, as if the person speaking was standing in the same room with me. This rarely happens, so it stunned me. I stopped and looked around. There was no one present who could have spoken those words. I began to research exactly *what* the Father's business is. I started with the words Jesus spoke as a twelve year old when He stayed behind in the temple.

Jesus' parents found Him sitting in the temple talking with the teachers—experts in the Scriptures—amazing them with His understanding and comprehension of God's Word. Wondering why Jesus had remained behind in Jerusalem, His parents questioned Him. Jesus responded that they should have known He would "be about His Father's business."

In the Greek interlinear English text in the IGENT, Luke 2:49 says, "And he said to them: 'Why [is it] that ye sought me? Did ye not know that *in* the [affairs] of the Father of me it behooves to be me?' With a subtext starting under the word, *in*= I must be about my Father's business?"

The Greek words for, "it behooves to," means *I must,* i.e., of Me I must be Me. Making the verse read this way: "Did you not know that in the [affairs] of the Father of Me I must be Me." Jesus the Son must do His Heavenly Father's business. He must occupy the position for which the Father sent Him.

Jews taught their children the profession of their parents. They all worked in the family business. A son worked with the father. A girl followed her mother. Jesus' earthly father was a carpenter, and he taught Jesus the same profession. At age thirteen, Jewish children graduated from training school when they were bar mitzvah (for boys), bat mitzvah (for girls). Then the child, at the age of thirteen, had moral and religious responsibilities. Then they proceeded into apprenticeship in their parents' business until the age of thirty. So if, for example, the boy was called to be a scribe, at the age of thirteen, the boy went to Jerusalem to apply for admission to a school of a famous rabbi. After a sufficient period of internship, which bound the person by agreement to learn some trade or craft, he was solemnly admitted into office. There was a variety of functions that would allow failure or success as the young men took up the business they had been taught. After years alongside their parents and teachers who influenced them, they now initiated their own office of service or name for themselves at about the age of thirty (*Smith's,* pages 596–597, paraphrased).

This is why Jesus at twelve, but not yet thirteen, was found in the temple talking to the priests after the feast in Jerusalem. Called to be our High Priest, Jesus was not to be doing His earthly father's business, but His Heavenly Father's business. Born fully God and fully human (see Col. 2:9; Heb. 1:3; 2:14–18), he was *yet without sin* (Heb. 4:15), Jesus knew He was here for a purpose and had an assignment to accomplish. He understood that soon He should be with the rabbi for further training. Setting His face in that direction, He proceeded to associate with those who were in full service to God. Jesus desired to learn from a knowledgeable priest, but discovered He already knew the God of Truth more than they did.

We too are to be about our Heavenly Father's business. Without an intimate relationship with God, an understanding of His character, and practical hands-on application and empowerment by the Holy Spirit, Christians cannot effectively do the business of the Kingdom of Heaven.

Our training and internship are vital tools of preparation for our assignment and purpose on the earth.

Scripture tells nothing about the preparation time of Jesus after leaving Jerusalem that day with His parents. Yet, we get clues from the preparation process Moses, David, and Paul went through. Each of them was trained by the Holy Spirit in seclusion and away from the public eye. Having left all of His glory in Heaven, Jesus practiced and worked along with the great Counselor, who also taught Him, just as He teaches us. All those obscure years, the Holy Spirit of Truth trained His senses and honed His faith as he went in obedience and had miracles accompanying Him. Later, the Scripture takes up the life of Jesus, now thirty, as He sets His face to do all the things His Heavenly Father had already planned for Him to complete. That is in the Writings (the Scriptures) and through the prophets.

Jesus knew that the business and affairs of His Heavenly Father awaited him. His occupation would be to manifest publicly Heaven on earth. The scope of their business was then as it is today, of great variety covering every aspect of life and death. It spanned the realms of kings, the elect, and all the way down to the poor and outcast of society.

We know that Jesus, like David, Abraham, and Job, died full of years. In dying at thirty-three, Jesus knew He had completed with excellence all matters assigned to Him. Having fulfilled His reason and purpose, Jesus, who came to do the business of His Father (see John 17:4), said on the cross, "It is finished!" As High Priest, He alone could examine and approve the sacrifice done in perfection (Lev. 4, *Smith's* pages 247–249, 577–579, and 633–634). He alone could select and train others to carry on the Father's work, in whose employment every Saint has a part.

A ROYAL MANDATE

In the Hebrew language, there are several meanings for the word "business."

1. Business is to labor or work and to have a position of trust and authority for duty or service. It is to hold an office, for example, to do the work of the porters; being involved in affairs of service. Also, the effect that the work produces is business, the fruit of what has been and will be done. Also associated with business is

the rustic labor of agriculture, as in the handling of implements in labor to produce something, as the fruit of righteousness that is produced. Business has two sides. One produces in its employment what is *evil business,* that is such as is of little profit like injustice. The other nature of labor is that of *good business* that is of great profit, such as the multiplicity of business or Godly standards.

2. "Business" also means "word," and that in context means, "the plural of all those words," and, "an eloquent man who has words, speech, and discourse." He is able to speak and persuade others. In Isaiah 22:23, Jesus is referred to as being as firm as a tent *peg.* His words will nail a person. It is especially a promise or a precept—an edict like a royal mandate. This work can be a rumor, counsel, or even a proposal of a plan."

3. Business may also be rendered, "what is the measure of his strength."

4. Words are how humankind communicates and produces a desired result, showing the power and weight of language. Words must have the occupation of actions performed, commentaries, or journals; hence a daily matter.

5. "The content of business has to do with a cause, a reason, or account of. Business deals with a place to which anything is sent or affairs that needs to be transacted" (Emphasis mine, throughout, paraphrased).

This makes it easier to see why Jesus, "The WORD" (see John 1:1–18), is all about the Father's business. God sent His Word, Jesus, who only does that which He hears from His Father. ". . . so is my word that goes out from my mouth: It will not return to me empty, but will accomplish what I desire and achieve the purpose for which I sent it" (Isa. 55:11).

As Saints, we are here to occupy until our bridegroom Jesus comes. By direct order from Jesus, we are not to sit on the sidelines. Rather, we are to be actively occupying (see Luke 19:13). Believers should not sit quietly on their couches or in their recliners watching the world go by. We are to be players in the affairs of the world. We are road signs to bring hope to the lost and dying, directing them to the foot of the cross. More mature Saints are to love and help those who are growing in the knowledge of the Lord.

FATHER

The word "father" only has one extensive definition in Hebrew. It means: Any ancestor, the founder, an inventor of something like the inventor of music; it is the author/maker which has been instituted with the love and care of a father. Honor is due a father; the father is one who brings up, or is a nourisher who bestows his benefits on those under his care. As in Job 29:16, "I was a father to the needy," and the Messiah is called eternal Father (of the people) in Isaiah 9:6.

It is the father's place to instruct his children as the teacher, just as Jesus has sent us the Counselor to teach us all things (see John 14:26). The connotation of father is also as the Master, Papa, Pope, and the Most Holy Father. The word "father" is especially significant when talking about the father of the king, or the father of the land or kingdom. It is the importance of the name given to his supreme counselor or possessor, and it is used to express intimate connection and relationship. Father denotes one who is endued with or excels in something, such as the father of peace (paraphrased throughout). The Father is the originator of peace, not only because He possesses peace, but also because He is our head, our Creator, our Counselor, and our Commander-in-Chief.

Our Father in Heaven wants to be more than invisible and distant. He desires to be our Father in every real aspect of life—not in the sense of worldly fathers, because none compares to our Father in Heaven. Even His name is holy. God is God, no one is like Him, and none can compare to Him. So, when we compare Him to human fathers, we have made God appear small. All human fathers are in a fallen state, so not one of them is like God (see John 10:30; 17:11, 22). We are made in His image. We need to know Him, and we must die daily and become Holy as He is.

Jesus sent the Counselor to instruct and teach us all truth and righteousness. As Christians submit and bow to His authority, we do the business of Heaven in excellence while Jesus fights on our behalf.

While on earth, Jesus displayed the Father's business. He was employed in demonstrating the chosen fast, defined here in Isaiah 58:6–7. "Is not this the kind of fasting I have chosen: to loose the chains of injustice and untie the cords of the yoke, to set the oppressed free and break every yoke? Is it not to share your food with the hungry and to provide the poor wanderer with shelter—when you see the naked, to clothe him, and not to turn away from your own flesh and blood?"

The chosen fast is to occupy Christians every day. Our employment is nestled in this deed. As we passionately pursue Jesus, and because we are His passion, Jesus wants our participation as we learn and share authority with Him.

We seldom think of the assignments in the chosen fast that we should be doing. By not doing them, we give huge areas of merchandizing of humankind to the enemy, who wants to keep everyone marginalized and trapped in incompleteness. Our work involves going out into the byways, areas seldom traveled, and the heavy traffic of the thoroughfares, asking and persuading all to come in to the wedding banquet, so that God's House will be full (see Matt. 22:9). We engage in spiritual warfare as we lean not on our own understanding, but trust in our Father in Heaven.

Those called by His name are to seize the moment. This is a vital activity, a war is fought in the employment of the Kingdom of Heaven. "The creation waits in eager expectation for the sons of God to be revealed" (Rom. 8:19), and to occupy, taking back property, doing business until He comes. Jesus is violent about the Father's business. We are to be like Him, passionate about the Kingdom of Heaven existing in our lives here on earth as it exists in Heaven.

- The enemy has marginalized my identity in Christ. How can it be restored?
- Employed in the Father's business, what is my job?
- In what ways am I doing the chosen fast?

Chapter 4

A CASE OF LOVE

My son, do not despise the LORD's discipline and do not resent his rebuke, because the LORD disciplines those he loves, as a father the son he delights in.

—Proverbs 3:11–12

BECAUSE OF HIS love, God tests us. Not because His love needs testing, for His love for humankind is everlasting. Rather He tests Believers to establish them in holiness and purity. Because of the persuasiveness of the enemy, the testing or trials that we go through refines and strengthens us into vessels that will not yield to evil. Because of the Lord's Holiness, His bride will be presented to Him without spot or wrinkle so that both of them are worthy of praise.

King David desired God's presence with him in Jerusalem. He loved God but was not knowledgeable enough to ask the correct procedure for moving the ark of God (see 2 Sam. 6). Since childhood, the Counselor/Spirit of Truth had advised him, and perhaps David thought that he understood the ways of the Lord. Therefore, David decided to proceed in a manner that in humankind's sight was prestigious and noble.

He planned a magnificent and glorious procession. Undoubtedly, lines of spectators would admire the ark as it made its way from the house of Abinadab to its destination in Jerusalem. The brand-new cart was impressive. It certainly could hold the weight of the ark. The oxen, freshly bathed and groomed, were arrayed with polished harnesses inlaid with gold ornaments. Flowers and brightly-colored ribbons adorned both the animals and the cart. This event was going to be the most elaborate in the nation. There would be dancing, music, and plenty of food. The parade would be glorious!

However, when they moved the ark in a manner that pleased humankind, a breach was produced and the ark started to fall over. To steady it, one of the men, Uzzah, touched the ark, and the mere contact killed him, because only the priests who were set aside to do service to the Lord could come near to God's Presence. Holiness broke out on the unconsecrated. Uzzah's death scared King David. This unexpected event brought everything to a standstill and tested the fiber of the self-reliant king. Terrified, David left the ark of the Lord at the house of a Gentile for three months and the Lord blessed Obed-Edom the Gittite while the ark was at his house.

Through testing and punishment, we become acquainted with God (see Heb. 12:6). No matter a person's rank, we all go through the refining fires of purification to remove all dross. David felt punished in his effort to do this good deed of returning the ark. He *now* ran to his Comforter/Holy Spirit, the one he could lean upon for trustworthy advice. Tragedy forced David to seek correction. He turned his mind toward God and the security of His instructions. David matured by studying, inquiring, and investigating to find out the correct course to bring God's Presence to Jerusalem.

Gods' heroes of the past and present learned that entering into God's presence haphazardly could produce undesired results. It is either God's way or a disaster happens, because darkness and light are opposites. When God visits humankind, it is with grace and mercy so that he can prune His children. Training up children in the way they should go takes times of discipline. Each time may consist of different forms of chastisement. I was one of six children. My parents chose to deter their children and to correct our destructive direction with a variety of necessary disciplines. I remember, because the times of punishment have given me a happier heart and healthier lifestyle today.

Can you relate to the way parents love their children enough to correct them from wrong ways and where evil leads? At the time, discipline seems harsh. It is never pleasant, but it leads to a harvest of righteousness and peace (see Heb. 12:11). Righteous acts cannot fellowship with unrighteous works. For this reason Holy and unholy cannot exist together, so either repentance occurs or disaster happens.

God's correction comes because we are His children. The correct way to walk is to follow His direction in our life. His commandments are the light that guides our feet and brings life to those that love His law (see Psa. 119:104–105, 163, 165). Caring for us far beyond the instruction and discipline of human parents that we might be partakers of His holiness (*Young's* lit. un-earthliness, see Heb. 12:10), God corrects or prunes those He loves that we might be fruitful children (see John 15:2).

GOD VISITS

In reading the Old Testament, I have noted that whenever God visited humankind, it resulted in correcting the direction they were traveling. Even in the beginning with Adam and Eve, who were hiding and covering themselves because they had gone in the wrong direction after sin, God came and corrected and punished them. Then, He brought comfort. Saints cannot come near to God without finding that correction is required. To come near to holiness, one either worships or repents. God is not an ogre (monster) waiting for us to do wrong. Rather, He is longing for us to be what He first designed us to be, made in His image. God gives power and grace, as He inspects our lives, to be able to bow to correction, for His holiness is pertinent to the lack of our holiness. However, God desires for His chosen to live in an atmosphere of security of mind, no matter where they live physically. We are to "make every effort to live in peace with all men and to be holy; without holiness no one will see the Lord" (Heb. 12:14).

No matter how wondrous the things of humankind are, or how inventive and persuasively presented, we must begin to change our thinking to what God's Word says. The act of confessing God's Word applies brakes to the wrong direction we are traveling, and the refining fire of God's love changes Saints without condemning them.

OUT OF FEAR COMES SERVICE

Because of my terrible fear of humankind, I was very timid. I would rather fail the assignment than stand in front of the class. Because of this fear of public speaking, I started praying for boldness to speak out for Jesus and His Kingdom. In 1999, before going on a mission trip to Korea, the Lord set me to reading the books of Samuel. The second time through, the character of Saul witnessed to me strongly that I was really like Saul, who was more reverent to what humankind thought than he was fearful of the Living God. As God touched my heart, I cried all the way through First and Second Samuel saying, "I am just like Saul." With discipline and the comfort of the Holy Spirit, the revelation of the Lord came to me—that I do not have to be like Saul! I can be like David! This became my heart's cry! Acknowledging this revelation required a violent stand against the old self-life. Kneeling before God, I humbly begged for change, because all things are possible with God (see Matt. 19:26). By pursuing becoming like Jesus, it is mine to possess. You too can be like Jesus; just go for Heaven and hold on.

Change takes discipline and loyalty. It takes courage, violent faith, and actions. Transformation takes knowing God's standards and ordinances. Christians need ears that hear what the Holy Spirit says; our senses need training and we need to mature in discernment. This is an inheritance for all Believers. Are we going to care what man says, or what the One True God says? Go after the God of Truth! For those Saints who care enough to seek Him, He allows us to find Him. Made in His image, we enjoy it when someone lovingly pursues us. God says that if we will seek Him with *all* our heart to *understand*, we will find Him (see Deut. 4:29). It only takes a little zeal on our part. When we wanted to learn to drive a car and pass the driver's test, it took the effort of continuous study, practice, and correction. Perhaps we failed, then tried again, and finally learned.

Those who know God recognize His correction and willingly humble themselves and accept the discipline of the Lord who loves us (see Prov. 3:11–12). In doing so, they are kissed by God (see Song of Solomon 1:2–4). As I discovered these Scriptures, I was in awe to think that God would give a mortal like me a kiss if I would turn to His reproof and be upright. That was a little perplexing at first because I thought, *How do I enjoy God's correction?* The answer is to enjoy God's correction by not rejecting it. If the correction is not to tell a little white lie, then stop, even if little white lies seem harmless. No lie can help. Only error comes from lies. It spreads through us like leaven, and a little leaven leavens the whole dough (see 1 Cor. 5:6–8). I started disciplining myself, which required either asking forgiveness, keeping my mouth shut, or just telling the truth, but in love.

The closer we draw to God's Truth, the brighter His fire becomes. We are to obey and leave behind the old nature as we grow in righteousness and please God. God's character is such that, unlike a man, He does not lie (see Num. 23:19). Truth and untruth cannot coexist, because the lie taints the truth. God tells the truth, and His truth is life.

As the Holy Spirit purifies us, testing continues to reveal wrinkles and spots that give us opportunity to die to our self-life. That produces our rewards of emotional health as we stop feeling deprived, rejected, dumped on, and oppressed. When we accept the reproof and direction of the Lord, we start doing what God says. "So in everything, do to others what you would have them do to you, for this sums up the Law and the Prophets" (Matt. 7:12). Thinking of others as more important than self is a huge trial. The needs of humankind are endless, and the revelation of them all-encompassing. The hardships in life fill every spectrum. When there is sickness, there is the need for healing prayer and anointing of the individual. Hardships in finance or emotion need remedies also. Wouldn't you like help to be released from this type of trap or bondage? In all things, there is the need to change our mindset and be alert to the needs of others. Whatever is in our own hand needs to be used to help others in the same way we would like to be helped. Recognizing what is real help to others takes effort. It is more than just saying, "Oh, that's too bad, or I'll pray for you." Pray, yes, but meet the need if it is in your power to do so (see Prov. 3:27–28). To be able to help and not do it, is sin.

When things in life get tough or are hard and we are without relief, Jesus is right there. He will never leave or forsake us. When we cry out to Him, He hears and answers, rescuing us from the grip of the problem. When the enemy knocks on our door, we can call out to Jesus, and He will come and answer our door!

> "Because he loves me," says the LORD, "I will rescue him; I will protect him, for he acknowledges my name."
>
> —Psalm 91:14

LIFE EXPERIENCE

The following experience will show a sample of the ways God works in our lives and how we respond. While waiting in the dentist's office, I sat next to a woman and her husband. Our conversation turned to things of healing. The room was small, so everyone heard our conversation as I told of my vacation with family. Alyssa, my grandniece, who as a child saw into the spiritual realm, became sick. Alyssa and I were sharing a room at night. In the early morning, we moved to the living room, thinking Alyssa might feel better sitting upright than lying flat. Trying to comfort her, I asked if I could pray for her. She said, "Jesus is sitting right there." She looked in front of her and sort of to the side of me. She said she had asked Him to heal her, and He was just sitting there. At a loss, but probably inspired by the Holy Spirit, I responded, "Jesus sometimes wants us to know that He is with us through the sickness."

The woman in the dentist's office to whom I was speaking inquired, "Why does He do that?" To answer her question, I continued with the story. After we had returned home, Alyssa's mother got sick. Alyssa knew she needed to be with her mother through that time. Her own sickness had helped her, a ten year old, understand that even if healing does not occur right away, Jesus is still with us. The woman and her husband rose to pay their bill at the counter. As the clerk talked to them about their bill, the women was saying something about Mayo. I didn't know what *Mayo* meant (my error of not really listening closely). I later realized that it may have been the Mayo Clinic and one of them needed more than dental work. Before I realized what was being said, it was too late. They were out the door and crossing the courtyard. I had missed the opportunity of asking if they wanted prayer.

This time I failed the test—though with God you just keep taking the test until you pass. I said a prayer for their needs and asked that the Holy Spirit would provide a more sensitive and courageous Believer in their future to speak with them. I just needed to trust that God had put me there at the right time to build their faith. In addition, I prayed that as I mature, I will have a keener awareness to the prompting of the Holy Spirit.

Yes, as we grow in the Word of God and start to digest what God has for us, we begin to live, talk, and breathe in a different way. We become doers of the Word and not just hearers. It is then we find that the things of the kingdoms or systems of the world will grow strangely dim in importance, and the things of the Kingdom of God will grow brighter and more genuine.

VESSELS OF WORTH

In the fires of affliction, Believers are often tried. Believers become a bride poured out and made spotless and holy through testing and purging. The process makes a vessel worthy of carrying great weight. Christians are refined by fire, made as pure as gold in our attitudes, language, and our way of life. God is purifying our nature, the mettle of our character. In doing so, He separates us as a people unto Himself. We are a people transformed into His image and conformed to His nature. Christians are called and chosen to be part of God's family all over the world.

Because God's love endures forever and ever, He will not leave us or forsake us to our own ways. He is patient, kind, long-suffering, and merciful, knowing our frailty. He wants every good thing for His children. He is eager for them to inherit what only love can attain.

- In what ways have I taken a stand against evil?
- Pruning comes from a loving God. How have I responded?
- How have I studied, inquired and investigated God's ways for my life?

Chapter 5

UNPERCEIVED POWERS

AS I DISCOVERED the forcefulness of seizing territory for the Kingdom of God, I noticed the unobjectionable ways in which God used force. I noticed some of the actions of God's people and what Jesus did. By the use of normal things in life, Believers were able to redeem land from enemy control. My mind started to comprehend the shrewdness of God, and my understanding grew and developed as the Holy Spirit led me into the unacknowledged ways of violence. Come with me as we go into obscure territory.

FAITH

"The only thing that counts is faith expressing itself through love" (Gal. 5:6). The powerful act of trusting God cements reality for the valiant of Heaven's Kingdom. These valiant Saints have faith as the sure foundation on which they cut their teeth. They have teeth that chew the real meat of God's Truth and faith demonstrated through actions of unconditional love.

Unable to please God without faith, Saints must believe that He is, and they must trust that God rewards those who diligently seek Him. Experiencing the certainty of God's words, we ascend to a higher level of faith. As we mature in the firm belief that the Word of God is true, we mature from faith to faith. This empowers Saints to stand firm and trust in God alone! The faith that is near us, right in our mouth, is powerful as we publicly confess Jesus as Lord. Absolutely believing that God raised Him from the dead results in salvation and righteousness (see Rom. 10:9–10). As witnesses of what we know from experience, we overcome the enemy by our words and by the blood of Jesus. We do not overcome the adversary by loving our self-life. These are mighty acts in the supernatural and go almost undetected in the visible world.

FAITH AND ACTION

Not always easily seen, violent faith often goes undetected in its power to seize possession as in this story in Genesis 23. The story surprised me because of its semblance to normal conversation. Here, an inconspicuous seizing of property takes place in the story of Abraham when he bought a piece of land to bury his wife, Sarah (Gen. 23:19, 49:32). Scripture later says that he took it by force. By the use of words, he fought for the land. The bargaining that went on seems like nothing. In fact, in the beginning, the owner told Abraham that the cave was his. He wanted to give it to Abraham (Gen.23:11). Now, wouldn't you be like me and think that God had just blessed you with the wealth of the heathen with this gift? This act of appropriation is violent because Abraham said no, he preferred to pay the full price for the parcel. The man responded that the piece of land was worth only a little bit of money to him. "Just take it and bury your wife," he said.

However, Abraham *insisted*. He was vehement that he would do nothing less than pay. When the owner lightly says the price, Abraham *seizes* the moment and pays the *full price* (Gen. 23:16, 25:10, 49:30). This little bit of barter over an insignificant piece of property is the fight Abraham wins and gains the first possession in the Promised Land. "You see that his faith and his actions were working together, and his faith was made complete by what he did" (James 2:22).

FORCEFUL LISTENING

Luke 6:27 (*CJB*) says, "Nevertheless, to you who are listening, what I say is this . . . ." Only those who are listening will be sons of God. There is the need to hear Jesus, as He alone is to have our ears. We must understand what His words say in order to judge what is right or wrong. Our ears are like scales of a balance that weigh one influence with the counteracting weight of another. As we intently listen and weigh words against what we understand, our opinions are formed. Often, the noise that comes into our ears weighs heavily on the side of the adversary, bending our thinking in the way of evil. Knowledge of God's Word is extremely important as Christians who know it can weigh it against the words of the world. They can judge between the true and the false and choose to stand either in truth or falsehood.

As His sheep, Christians are to know the voice of the Holy Spirit. We are to listen to ascertain God's voice, His instructions, and then to quickly obey. Christians are not to obey the instruction of a stranger. Remember just say "no" to the voice of a stranger, a person who does not know God intimately. Sheep do not travel faster than their Shepherd. So, do not be in a big hurry and run ahead of God. Those who are learning are not above the teacher. They let Him lead, and they do not become transgressors by stepping beyond what God has said.

Learning is a progression, so if we have been listening to strangers who are not part of the family of God—strangers who are not free to do and say what God does or says—we must turn and walk in the direction God is going. Right now is the time to recognize what may be the *voice of a stranger* in our life. Here are some of the places where we hear strangers or get the world's words: our favorite movie star, our best friend, our spouse, our peers, and the daily news. A stranger's voice could be from heroes of the world, such as Darwin or Dr. Spock or other worldly scientists. We need to recognize the spiritual voice of the enemy. To learn to distinguish between voices, we need our ears trained in discernment. We need to major in knowing the voice of the Holy Spirit, which can be confirmed by the Word of God. We are to test the spirits to see if they are from God (see 1 John 4:1). Then we shall have the peace that passes understanding.

Ezekiel 12:2 reveals that the rebellious have ears but do not hear and eyes but do not see. Often Christians hear, but what they hear just goes in one ear and out the other, having no lasting effect. For our hearts to understand the words of life, they must first resonate in our thinking as we ponder and meditate upon the Word of God. We must weigh words on the scales of God's just and right standards that reside in us.

When the Holy Spirit spoke to our hearts, He watered our measure of faith; we accepted Jesus as Savior. Our life turned to follow Him. This simple act of repentance—the turning of our mind—is an extreme blow against the forces of darkness. Death's grip is broken. The doors are flung open, and the light of truth shines into our life! A Christian is born and becomes known in the supernatural.

In the parable in Matthew 13 where the sower scatters his seeds/words on the ground/people, the birds ate it, the cares of the world destroyed it, and some seeds/words planted in poor soil/people went right back into

darkness. Attacked and tricked by enemies, those who start to believe
fall from the truth. However, those who do simple acts of acceptance,
grow and move through events in life using violent acts of aggression
against the dark side. Holding on to faith in Jesus is powerful. When a
person comes to the side of light, he or she appropriates truth instead
of lies. They move from the camp of death to the camp of life. You may
have thought that death camps started with Hitler. They didn't. The
death camps started after Adam and Eve sinned and God sent them out
of Eden. The whole world became a death camp—sin's plague of death
on people. By the small act of listening to the Holy Spirit and responding,
Jesus comes into our heart and we gain freedom. At this point, though,
we might not understand in its entirety the scope of what has happened.
It outweighs destruction in our life in a portion unknown to us but heavy
in the supernatural realms.

The scales now tipped toward the Kingdom of Heaven, we are free
to listen intently to its ways. The new Christian is put into an unknown
environment, and without further guidance and fellowship with more
mature Believers, he or she can remain a babe, easily fall away from faith
completely, or be dwarfed in spiritual growth. Like Peter on the Mount of
Transfiguration, they may want to honor other famous men of God, but
the Father in Heaven says, "This is my Son, whom I have chosen; listen
to him" (Luke 9:35). Jesus is the only one we are to hear and esteem.

LESSONS

Upon discovering some missing elements in my life about knowing
Jesus, I decided I needed to pay attention to these truths. The first
startling revelations came in a time of heavy anguish in my life. It was
then that I ran to the Scriptures for comfort and guidance. These times
of desperation tell of my development into a new creation as I intently
listened to Jesus my Lord. One of the first things I discovered was this
truth: The correct direction to run is toward God.

Another huge revelation to me came a few days later when the NAME
of Jesus became real. He was no longer distant in a manner of speaking,
but brought over against me. This revelation rocked my world! It would
be some years before I would be in a position to use just the name "Jesus"
to repel the presence of demons.

This name—JESUS—is powerful! Even when whispered, it is
effective. Nothing can defeat this name . . . nothing! Get into the habit
of saying "Jesus," because as we practice saying it, do not just think it,

but speak "Jesus" out of our mouth, we bring Him to the front of our thoughts. We must practice what is necessary to be able to use His name when needed. Do not think His name will just spring out of our mouth. When accidents happen or terror strikes, it will overtake us if we do not immediately put the weight of the name of Jesus against it. Our mouth and heart must have the habit of saying His name. We have a responsibility to train our ears to hear how the Holy Spirit is moving and to recognize what God wants done. We must be careful not to let anything terminate our effectiveness. By desiring wisdom and the knowledge of the Holy One, we willingly turn our will toward God.

Jesus said to everyone who has ears, "Let him hear," meaning it is possible to hear the words of God whether in the natural or in the supernatural. The same words found in Mark 4:23 advise us to consider them carefully! For by the measure that we hear it will be measured back to us, and even more. We have the promise that anyone who starts to listen and understands a little will receive more understanding, but the one who does not listen to understand, has what he heard taken away.

In Daniel 5, King Belshazzar was *weighed in the balances and found lacking*. God was listening to him. God weighed what he said and did and found no substance. The young king soon died and the kingdom was left to others.

What voices influence us? That which weighs heavily in our heart will come out of our mouth (see Matt. 15:18–20). How are we influencing those that hear us? Think about it—for God is listening.

REMEMBRANCE

The encouragement of other Believers is important as we build each other up in our faith. Remembering what Jesus has done in our life and what He has done in times past strengthens our confidence in what He will do in the future. With these things, we encourage others.

When having communion, Jesus commanded Saints to "Do this in remembrance of Me." In this, we remember who Jesus is and the experience of what He has done in our life and what the witnesses testify of and history confirms. This establishes a foundation of trust for the Believer. Building memories on the same mind of faith that Jesus has, Saints will stand firm. It is not by might or by power, but by the Spirit that we will survive. Trusting God's amazing grace is a simple, clear truth to keep in mind.

To call to remembrance, and to encourage and strengthen Believers, we testify to the following event: In Mexico, the Holy Spirit sent the missionary David Hogan to the home of one of his associate pastors to pray for the pastor's wife. Unknown to the missionary, the wife had suffered with bleeding tumors for months. Now, extremely weak, she was at the brink of death, even after receiving much prayer. She asked her husband to send for the missionary. Not knowing it, David was already on his way under direction from God. Both the pastor and the missionary had already experienced mighty miracles in ministry. The missionary arrived, and when he evaluated her condition, he received discernment from the Holy Spirit. He did not immediately pray for the woman. He first took the husband into the kitchen, and as they had coffee, he began recounting the many miracles that each of them had seen—that God had produced through their hands. After an hour or so, the husband said, "OK, I'm ready." They both laid hands on his wife and Jesus healed her. Immediately, she rose and asked if the missionary was hungry. Good manners demand that you never refuse a meal. He said yes, and she hurried out to kill a chicken and prepare a meal to set before their guest.

Believers need to tell of the power of God. God is still on His throne and still does wonders. We appreciate this story, but it becomes real only when we are in the same place. There is effort and commitment to pray for people we know and do not know. However, when sickness and death are taking the life of intimate friends or family, not wavering in the prayer of faith takes on a new level of meaning (see James 5:15). For Believers, *remembering the extraordinary things of God* is a necessity.

God will help us begin and continue living in strength in every condition in which we find ourselves. Believers can have peace and rest in God even when things crumble in our lives. Because of oppressors, we are to remember that the Lord will send a Savior, a Champion, a Mighty One. He will deliver us! God hears our heartfelt cry and remembers us. This alone is enough to make us joyous. If God is not the One who saves us, who would? Not the adversary. He wants to marginalize our existence and maximize our demise.

The challenge is to lay aside reliance on humankind and remember that God is in control of all things. When this challenge is accomplished, it eliminates many struggles. By this unseen force of bringing to remembrance daily the things He has done for us, Believers put God in the highest place in our thoughts. We can remember such things as the country we live in is not perfect, but in which we are free to do almost anything. Here in the United States, we have so much, and at present, we live in relative quietness and safety. We have much to be thankful for, and so far we are free to extol the Holy name of Jesus.

There are endless things to thank God for each day. God has brought us through many difficult things in our life . . . we did get through them. Start today with at least one thing for which you can praise God and add to it, enlarging the memory of His kind intentions toward us. Christians are to thank Him in all things, making his blessings known to all humankind. If we don't thank Him, we tend to think we did it all on our own. We may say, "Well, we did it! We worked hard. We took care of our health, our family. This business was our idea." Yes, we did our part, but do not forget that God did His part. There is a sharing of accomplishment with the Creator of Heaven and Earth who made the rain to fall on the earth that produces and sustains life. Humankind would have no life without food, water, and air. Or perhaps, we could have been born in another land and may not have had the opportunity to go to school, or not have had the opportunity to make enough money on which to live. The good business idea was His in the first place. We realize the frailty of our health when disease attacks us. God holds our breath and gives and takes it at His set time. The rest are just fringe benefits. Praise Him for them.

There is so much more that the Father wants us to have, so go for the whole thing! Our loving God is not stingy. He is a giver and He wants to give it all to us. Awakening to our destiny, we freely die to self that Christ might live *big* in us. This is an act of violence.

Passionate Christians see the need to be aggressive in life. We need to let Jesus live big in us by allowing Jesus to reign in more than just a small corner of our life. By letting God out of the box that we keep Him in, we come to maturity and grow up in God. Do not let Jesus remain the same in us as when we first knew Him. He is not the babe in the manager. That picture keeps Him helpless and dependent. Nor is He still on the cross dying for our sins—the image of the sacrificial lamb. Realize that He is alive! See Jesus as the King above all kings—the Lion King! Understand that He is mighty! He is coming again to judge the living and the dead. Recognize that He wins!

OPPORTUNITY

If you are as I am, you have found that it is easier to do anything than change. I would rather work, listen to a preacher or a CD, or watch television or listen to the radio than try to change and have a relationship that struggles with the demands of intimacy and removing self from its pedestal. It is easier for us to talk about such a life than to walk it out. To live it and do it successfully is much harder. Christians have an opportunity to possess a piece of the Promised Land as we speak up in normal conversation and fight against the forces of evil that try to take over this world. It takes aggressive action against the fears of our nature and character as the Holy Spirit leads us.

By simple acts of faith, listening, and remembering, we will know who God is and that Jesus has all power and authority. Knowing how powerful the Kingdom of Heaven is and by using the mighty NAME of Jesus in everyday life, we will bring a steady increase on the road to our recognition as one *not of this world* but of the Kingdom of Heaven.

- By faith and actions, how have I placed God in the highest place?
- What is the first place I run to for comfort?
- What remembrances of Jesus have I told to others?

Chapter 6

FIVE WERE LEFT—
CONSEQUENCES?

GOING FORWARD IN the knowledge of the Kingdom of Heaven and learning to understand more of God, I soon found that He led my times of study, just as He did when I studied the subject of keeping God's Laws. The Holy Spirit took me by the way of grace. Other times the Spirit would start revealing certain truths in Scripture. You know He's come when what you read makes your throat tighten and tears come. Or while reading, you say, "Oh, wow! Look at that!" Such was the case when I discovered that I feared God less than my parents and the rules they taught me, and even less than I feared my peers and friends. Since I knew God as a God of love, He was pretty much at the end of reverence in my life.

During that year in my seeking God, He proved to me that He *doesn't fight fair*. He uses things beyond humankind's ability to fight and win. When I came across evidence of His awesome power, I marked the margin of my Bible with *God doesn't fight fair*.

Christians cannot begin to have wisdom until we fear the God of wisdom (see Prov. 9:10). To honor God above all others in holy fear is of great benefit to us. All Scripture is true and breathed of God Himself. Understanding this should give us fearful respect. The Writings tell us that because of the hardness in the hearts of humankind, past events prove that God has acted justly and will act again. Those who shine brightly for Jesus understand that God is worthy to hold the highest place of honor and to receive all glory from them. They know that what He says is true, so they do not bow to serve another entity, but love and serve Him alone.

God Will Not Always Strive with Humankind

The LORD saw how great man's wickedness on the earth had become, and that every inclination of the thoughts of his heart was only evil all the time. The LORD was grieved that he had made man on the earth, and his heart was filled with pain.

—Genesis 6:5–6

There have been times when humankind has become so corrupt, and the pain in God's heart becomes so great, that He says, "It is enough!" Humankind's hardness toward God comes when we do not fear the Lord. In Proverbs 1:29, it states that there is no fear of the Lord because humankind hates knowledge. In a time when knowledge is set on a pedestal of humankind's making, it needs to be understood that *humankind hates the knowledge that is from God.* Unaware that their hearts have hardened toward their Creator, people live their own way. Their necks stiff, they think that every day is the same as the one before, so they continue to forget God. With humankind's denial of Him, they conclude that God is in Heaven and does not care about them. However, such rebellious desires led to the following events in the history of the human race. The occurrences could have unfolded something like this:

First came the end of an age, in the wickedness in Noah's day, when no rain fell because the whole earth was watered by springs (see Gen. 2:5–6). When a day comes that will be like no other, the day starts out normal, but soon humankind notices a startling change as the sky becomes frightful and mysterious. "Look there! There is some kind of darkness rising out of the north." "What is that?" As people gather, they agree that no one has seen anything like this before, and it is freaking them out. "What's happening? Now the blackness is everywhere!" The sky looks angry—so threatening! The sky grows darker. Eerie noises multiply. Thunder roars! "Did you hear that?" Lighting streaks across the horizon! And for the first time ever, water falls from the sky!

Screams erupt from every person not on the ark. "Look at that. The earth's breaking open!" "Oh, no! Water's gushing out." The people of the earth frantically run for safety. To see the water pouring out of the sky and earth is a horror. "Help! Help! The sky is falling!" What a phenomenon. Has anyone seen anything like this? The floodgates have opened to pour out a watery wrath! The water roars as it spews out. In a moment water is ankle-deep and rising! They stare in amazement, and someone curses *the crazy* who has been declaring that God is sending destruction on the earth—you know, that crazy man who's building that huge monstrosity—that, that wooden thing!

"Oh, no!" As horrifying screams explode from humankind, they scramble to higher ground. Then they remember what Noah said. "Repent?" "What's repent? Was it one-hundred years that he begged us to turn from wickedness?" "We're not bad people. What wicked ways was he talking about? Life has always been this way, so changing is not an option. At least, not changing to be like that *nut case!*" In addition, the water keeps coming. It is waist deep and rising!

They had made fun of all the creatures that God brought to live in the ark Noah and his family built. They criticized Noah for gathering so much food. Then, a week ago, all activity stopped when *God shut the door* (see Gen. 7:16), leaving outside those who desired to continue to live life their way. Everyone except those inside the ark drowned as the deluge continued to pour out of the floodgates of Heaven and earth (see Gen. 7:11–12). The torrent of water covered the earth, rising twenty feet over the highest mountains.

Later in Genesis 19, we read the history of God's visit to Sodom and Gomorrah. Wickedness resided in these two cities, but so did righteous Lot and his family. Their home had been in Sodom for many years. Even though the citizens were weirdoes, doing all manner of perversion, each person turning to evil acts—man with man, woman with woman, and every other kind of wickedness. They did not regard God; they were stiff-necked and their hearts were hard. They relished immorality, selfish ambition, and their pride piled high. All their deeds were bad in the sight of the Lord. Evil had become so commonplace that they believed it to be moral and normal. God in His mercy sends two angels in the middle of the night to rouse and persuade six people to come out: Lot, his wife, his sons-in-law, and his two daughters. The angels had to drag Lot, his wife, and their two daughters out. The sons-in-law remained. Because of unbelief, they continued to sleep.

The fireworks started when Lot's family was outside the city (see Luke 17:29). Fiery bombs fell out of the sky, exploding with suffocating fumes, and the smell of sulfur ascended into the air. All who lived in these two cities, with their cultic and traitorous ways, burned to ashes (see 2 Pet. 2:6). God had opened the doors of vengeance once again. This time fire and brimstone rained down from Heaven on the two cities until nothing was left—not one person lived. There wasn't one animal or green plant anywhere. The structures of the cities were decimated! Ruined! Everything destroyed!

Four leave the city, one looks back and turns to salt, so only three (half of the original six chosen to come out) live to tell the story of their escape.

From a distance, other cities and towns are panic-stricken at the terrible wonder as they hear the sounds and view the dreadful display of lights mixed with billowing smoke. They stare in horror and they wonder if anyone survived! Will they be next?

The history of the flood and the destruction of Sodom and Gomorrah are evidence that God sketches out the history of humankind. Both events confirm the promises of the fulfillment of last-day events before the return of Jesus Christ (see Luke 17:26–30; 2 Pet. 3:10–12). Just as today, wickedness abounds and even the people of God pay little attention. Everything seems to be the same. Humankind works and plays, eats and drinks, marries and gives in marriage (see Matt. 24:38), buys and sells and does business (see Luke 17:28). The storms come and go, and there are signs in the heavens and on the earth. There are wars and rumors of wars (see Matt. 24:6; Mark 13:7), famine strikes the land, and plagues dispatch death to the inhabitants of earth. Many Believers have lost their first love and are doing acts of licentiousness and idolatry. Reflecting the image of Jezebel, they do not look for the soon return of their Lord (see the churches in Rev. 2:1–3:16). Trusting in the power of the enthroned God is such a rare commodity, that in Luke 18:8 we are warned that, "When the Son of Man comes, will he find faith on the earth?" Beloved, it is time to examine ourselves to see if Jesus is in us (see 2 Cor. 13:5).

These judgments are due to humankind's corruption and are determined by the just and righteous God of truth. He has acted and will act again. The earth does not experience the time of visitation (judgment) without receiving many warnings and much mercy. God is extremely longsuffering. He loves humankind so much that He gives us ample opportunity to change our minds and to turn our hearts from wickedness and come to Him.

WHEN JESUS RETURNS

Finally, we find God's promises of what is to come. Jesus forewarns Believers of events that will take place when He returns (see Matt. 24:39–42). He tells of two men doing business: one is taken and the other is left. Two women are working, one is left the other taken. Together with the illustration of the ten virgins where five are taken and five are left, all three stories relate the consequences of very similar people—people who accept the gift of life. They appear to be Christians; however, there is something very important lacking, for half are left behind. All are vignettes of 50 percent left outside! Half!—The *door shut by God* once more.

Let's slow down and take a longer look at the story of the ten virgins. This story is so important that Jesus goes into great detail. It bears witness to how Believers are recognized. There are ten virgins, but only five of them kept extra oil on hand, and only these five go on into the wedding banquet—the Kingdom of Heaven (see Matt. 25:10). We need to understand more of the story, because we are the virgins in the story. We either enter or come to the closed door.

Parts of the English marginal text in IGENT in Matthew 25:1–13 (KJV) says:

> Then shall the Kingdom of Heaven be likened unto ten virgins, which took their lamps, and went forth to meet the bridegroom. And five were wise, and five were foolish. They that were foolish took their lamps, and took no oil with them: but the wise took oil in their vessels with their lamps. While the bridegroom tarried, they all slumbered and slept . . . at midnight . . . was a cry made, Behold, the bridegroom cometh; go ye out to meet him . . . [A]ll those virgins arose, and trimmed their lamps . . . the foolish said unto the wise, Give us of your oil; for our lamps are gone out. But the wise answered, . . . Not so; lest there be not enough for us and you: but go . . . to them that sell, and buy for yourselves.

Believers are the ten virgins who are carrying the revelation of Jesus and radiating light into the darkness of the world. They are charged to occupy until Jesus returns. They are satisfied that what they believe about the good news is all they need. Because Jesus is coming back, we will have to be alert and waiting, for we know neither the day nor the hour when He will come. The oil of the Lord's Spirit lights the lamp, which is the soul of a person. However, as decades pass, the brightness of the belief and trust in Jesus' return starts to wane. They began to slumber and others slept.

In church history, we read that the lamps' fires burned brightly at first, then the Dark Ages came. After those years of darkness, when people didn't even have Bibles, a revival took place in a restoration known in history as the Reformation. One by one in the assembly-place of God, tabernacle furniture was replaced. Throughout the ages, there are revival-seasons when another article is set in place in the Holy Place toward the Holy of Holies. As a remnant of zealous Saints blaze through the ages (see Rom. 11:4–5) as faithful witnesses, they overcome the adversary by the blood of the Lamb and by the word of their testimony; they do not love their lives so much as to shrink from death (see Rev. 12:11).

At the darkest time—midnight—the call rings out. It blasts the stillness of the darkness with the trumpet voice of the best man, "Make ready the way for the coming of the Groom. Go out and meet Him!" And the herald is heard saying, "Come Lord Jesus, come!"

All ten virgins seem to have a radiance to show to the world, but only half of them are wise; the other half are foolish. Only the Spirit of the Lord, who explores the recesses of the breast of humankind, knows the true lovers.

The ten stand up and trim their lamps, preparing their souls. Five lack the element of oil acquired by rubbing against the Holy Spirit and by spending time with Him. These five virgins fail the oil test, resulting in 50 percent of the Believers left behind!

Five are foolish, five are not. Proverbs gives understanding to the disposition of the wise and the foolish—those easily swayed. Starting in Proverbs 1 and going on through chapter 30, they (the foolish and the wise) are played off against each other. The foolish are simple and do not understand, nor are they prudent/shrewd; therefore, they grieve and hate their parents. They mock, seeking true wisdom, and tear down their own houses. Foolish people are quick-tempered and inherit folly, lacking judgment as they devour all they have. Even when danger is present, the fool keeps going and suffers.

They are killed by waywardness and destroyed by complacency as they will believe anything! Because of the things in the world coming against them, the foolish, who are the easily swayed virgins, wither, fade, and become weakened.

Because of the infiltration of impiety, they start to decay. Their light becomes dull. They are stupid with regard to God's Word. Because of their insincerity and lack of dedication to truth and righteousness, the worldly treat them with contempt. These Christians claim to be different, but they are common. They look just like the carnal person of the world. Confused, they mix the wickedness of the world with the righteousness of God's standards, becoming liberal and lax and not willing to take a stand or speak out for Jesus. Christians who are involved in immorality and other shameful acts do not recognize the waning of their flame. They no longer seek the counsel of God, and so they are emptied of the fire of real life. They have no real witness. They are fruitless and have lost sight of the purpose of life.

Confused by the language of the world, and regarding it as truth, these five foolish ones believe the boasting and perverse ideas of the world. They are ashamed of the Word of God. Their prophets lie and act as fools, speaking barbarously as they lead Christians astray. Ignorantly, they senselessly talk of what they do not know. Unskillful in the ways of Heaven, the five undiscerning virgins easily fell prey to carnal persuasion and were enticed by the ways of the world. They erred and went astray, *having a deceitful tongue.* They had eyes only for this world and its glory.

Unknowingly, the foolish put their souls in danger by not spending time in the Spirit, and that results in no extra oil in their flask. Now, time is lost, their oil is gone, and they are empty of discerning the inward voice of the Holy Spirit. They go to buy oil from those who sell, but it takes too long, and they return too late! Thud! *The door shuts!*

The wise, also described in Proverbs 1 and continuing chapters, take time to listen and add to their learning. With discernment, they know all the meaning of dark sayings. They turn to the Lord's reproof and wisely learn from Him. They are not wise in their own eyes, but are humble. They inherit honor by listening to their Father's instruction and gaining understanding. Rewarded for their wisdom, they are actively on the job in the Kingdom of Heaven. Knowing when and what to speak, they bring healing and gain favor. Their tree produces the fruit of life. They win souls. Building their house, they shun evil and fear the Lord. They bring joy and delight to their parents. They live among the wise who know discernment. As they increase in strength, they attack cities and pull down strongholds with God's great power. In wisdom, they keep themselves under control. Their judgments are fair as they give right answers and God kisses them!

The five wise virgins have plenty of oil. They shine brightly, remain fresh, and are new with zeal. They do not tire of the witness of Jesus and the ways of Heaven. Symbolically, the lamp for the oil is also called the wineskin for the new wine. The Holy Spirit gives the oil and new wine—oil for anointing and power. The new wine, called the elixir of life because it takes control of the head, changes our mind into a new creation of God. By the anointing oil supplied by the constant rubbing against the Holy Spirit, they have become the anointed ones—sons of oil (see Zech. 4:14) like Jesus, the Anointed One.

Adorned in fine, white linen vestures, the anointed ones live doing righteous acts (see Rev. 19:8). Believers, protected by the shield of faith and the sword of truth, do Kingdom business, and hopelessness is undone. The Lord inaugurates them as priests, prophets, and kingly vessels. They are sons of God. Their work in ministry is one of reconciliation—reconciling all things back to the Father.

Keeping themselves only for Jesus, the wise virgins have remained virtuous and are modest with all piety. In discernment, they skillfully use whatever gifts that have been given them to be ambassadors to the world. They are not ashamed of the gospel of Jesus Christ, and they use its power to save humankind (see Rom. 1:16). Prepared by the Holy Spirit in the wisdom and understanding of the One True God, they are prudent and consistently seek wise counsel.

Standing firmly for the truth and the righteousness of God, the five wise virgins do not yield to the tricks and persuasions of worldly people. They continue walking in love. Humbly, they fulfill God's purpose for life. Living water continually oozes from them, and they not only shine, but they also blaze as brightly as a lamp on a stand (see Luke 11:33–36). They wait expectantly for the return of Jesus. No matter the darkness, they are eager for His appearing.

PREPARATION TIME

The Living God talks with non-believers to move them to action. However, most of Scripture plainly states that God is usually talking to His people who are called by His name—those of us who are supposed to know Him.

Until the Kingdom of God is made evident in our lives in this world, it is our part to practice and show ourselves approved unto God (see 2 Tim. 2:15). Diligent Believers have a responsibility to be prepared and ready at any time to give an answer for the hope that is in us.

In *Webster's Dictionary* (1976), the partial meaning of "prepare" is, "to fit for a special purpose, make ready, as to *prepare* a room for occupancy; to make mentally ready." *Preparation* involves action! In the Greek, the word, "*prepare*" means to provide or make ready with fatness (anointing oil; emphasis mine)." Oil is needed for our lamps to brightly burn. The Holy Spirit who rubs or paints our mind with the purposes of God helps us.

The Holy Spirit covers us with colored layers of oil (*in Hebrew* see *Strong's* #7551, 7275 [3]), rubbing us as we submit to the Spirit of counsel and wisdom. This anointing shields us and gives us tenacity against the weapons of evil and offense so that the sharp darts the enemy throws at us do not penetrate. Wickedness stands off.

Proverbs 4 and 5 also explain that there is a wooing from two forces in a person's life. Two forces illustrated by two people named Wisdom and the Adulteress. These two supernatural forces beckon to all humankind in the marketplace of the world, trying to influence and persuade us to choose one or the other. Our choices will divide us into two groups. One joins the camp of the One True God, and the other group follows the father of lies.

There is disaster and ruin for those who know God but do not try to learn and prepare. They follow their own thoughts and desires. God ruins the disobedient. He makes them a dry waste place! Saints cannot go by what feels good or what the world is doing. Knowledge of the Holy One is first on the list of *things to do*. The wise virgins went by the Word of God and continued to persevere. They loved to do it God's way.

Living in the world, we are engaged in its turmoil. Nevertheless, Saints are to have inner peace, which is a different type of the *peace* than the world possesses. So many times, we Christians have turmoil in our lives because we claim to know God, but we have not done what He has said. Often we feel the Holy Spirit tug on our heart, but we do not turn in His direction, nor do we desire discernment to rid ourselves of carnal things of the world. Below is another clue as to why 50 percent stand outside the closed door. There is a warning, in the English (KJV) marginal text, of Luke 12:47 (IGENT), "And the servant, which knew his lord's will, and prepared not himself, neither did according to his will, shall be beaten with many stripes [meaning calamity]."

This verse talks of virgins who foolishly do not prepare themselves and gain calamity. Sit back and meditate on this verse and notice how loving the Lord is to tell us of His ways and how boundaries affect our life. As we read His word, we start to know a bit of God's thinking. We begin to understand how He acts, His attitudes, and His character. Presented with so many telling signs, can we tell if we know Him? If we fail to seek His wisdom and neglect to form a personal relationship with the Lord, we will not understand nor regard the certainty of God's Word. In failing to do so, we invite calamity into our life.

Saints who carry a heavy anointing go through great hardships without yielding in their trust in God. No matter the assault of the enemy, they remain faithful. It is different when the adversary attacks active Believers versus Believers turned over to torturers. In the latter case, by calamity, God tries to persuade them to correct their direction and turn their stiffened necks toward Him again, and if they refuse, it seems that they will stand on the wrong side of the closed door (see Matt. 25:30).

It's Time to Awake

There was a time when the ten slumbered and slept. To slumber or sleep does not mean what we might suppose. In Hebrew "to slumber" means "to be idle, especially through indolence and to be slothful." To sleep means "to be languid, weariness that causes a very great inertness without power to move, to act or resist." Therefore, we see that resistance is not futile. As a person is engaged in righteousness and justice, their efforts ward off the languid effects of the world's pull on our life. Christians who are awake and able to stand resist the attempts of the enemy to keep them asleep as they move forward with God.

As Saints determine to turn from old directions, even slightly, they start on the narrow way entering into the Kingdom of Heaven. True living is done with faces in direct line with the way God is going. Heavy weights such as fear, jealousy, dismay, bitterness, and every evil and wicked thing that we have carried around all through life, will lift off our shoulders. Many times, I have literally felt weight lift off me as I repented and asked for help. God does not change. He is no respecter of persons. What He does for me, He will do for each person.

What an eye-opener I have had and continue to have regarding God and the Kingdom of Heaven. His ways oppose my own culture and do not fit any other culture on earth. Salvation is free to all, but it costs to enter into God's *rest*. There is a price to pay to follow Jesus. It is work, and it does cost to except the humbling of the Lord and live free. But, it is worth the price!

The time has come to ask, will we go out to meet the Bridegroom in the street and dine at His banqueting table? Will people recognize us as being with Jesus? Or will we be seen as one of the foolish, who in desperation turns to seek oil too late, who misses the street celebration with the entourage of wedding guests? The choices are ours to make.

The loving mercy and grace of the Almighty God remind us of the truth of His words and actions. He tells us of events of coming judgment. Therefore, before the *door shuts* again *for that final time*, before the fire comes (see 2 Pet. 3:7), we still have time, for we are on this side of the last fire!

- How do I know stories in the Bible are real?
- Jesus is returning. How can I be waiting and alert?
- I am a lamp. How can I get extra oil?
- Do I understand that half of those who called themselves Christians will be left?

Chapter 7

RUDIMENTARY SKILLS

Anyone who lives on milk, being still an infant, is not acquainted with the teaching about righteousness. But solid food is for the mature, who by constant use have trained themselves to distinguish good from evil.

—Hebrews 5:13–14

MILK IS THE nourishment for babies as they remain in the playpen of life. When Believers remain on a diet of milk, growth does not happen. To grow, we must chew on the views of Heaven—meat must be in the diet. We must meditate and study to gain knowledge of God's right and just standards. Once we know what God's righteousness is, we can activate and experience the skills that help us acquire a genuine life here on earth. We can't just say we are Christian: Christians have an occupation to go and give words of encouragement and actions to help. Calming fears and anxieties does not just happen.

Before Saints can have a witness, they must observe something. Just as going through a test gives us a testimony, knowledge gives understanding, and doing gives experience in steps forward. We do not enter into something new and do it unless we are shown how. For instance, unless Believers learn that we can lay hands on those with infirmities and pray for them (see Jas. 5:15), we remain idle. Unless we trust that God can raise the dead, we cannot approach a dead person and try to speak a word of life to them.

By using God's Truth, we train our five senses according to the principles of Heaven. The elementary things all Believers should understand are knowing about sin, repentance, baptism, righteousness, and the resurrection. These are the basics we build upon. Maturity comes when we grow past these foundational truths and we become mature, meaning perfect, as Jesus is perfect/mature. As we mature, we become Sons of God—whether female or male.

The process includes becoming steadfast in the Word of God. Until our fear of man and our thoughts of failure are under our feet, the fear of death cannot be conquered in our heart (see Heb. 2:15). Everything takes practice. Christians who have healing and the dead raised in their ministry tell of having prayed for many, even hundreds of people whom God has not healed or raised to life. However, they know that it is up to God to do the *actual* healing or bring someone back to life. God's valiant ones do only the part they know how to do. They trust God for the outcome. Saints, we just need to do our part. When we are in a position to do the works of God and do not do them, it may be because things of the world rule in our mind. Some deeds that God wants us to do, such as expelling demons, healing, and raising the dead, come only with prayer and fasting (see Matt. 17:21, Mark 9:29).

What if we miss the opportunity? God will give another opportunity. He is patient in training His children. Unless God sends someone, a person will live in the bondage of infirmity, hunger, or whatever condition the person is in. Maybe it will be us who act on His behalf. Let's be bold, courageous, and deliver the oppressed—those who are being held down by the enemy. If a spirit of depression possesses them, pray. At least try to cast that spirit off of them. It may not happen; then again, it may. Keep praying. As we are faithful in little things, God will move. We are like doctors giving the ailing the healing power of Jesus. Each Believer can lay hands on the sick and pray—none of us are exempt. The sick cannot be healed unless Believers rouse themselves to come to their aid, letting Jesus flow through them. Do not hold Him for ourselves, but give Jesus to others. What does that mean—give? People are waiting for help. So, do not fear. As we release what we have in our hands, God will give us even more. He is the God of overabundance. Jesus always meets needs because He cares for people. God loves people. He loves all of humankind.

Be zealous for God. We must get violent with the old nature to cast down those thoughts that stop righteous actions. The elementary things in this world hold our attraction. So, if we are doing things our own way, *stop!* If you are loaning money to friends with interest, then stop. If you are gossiping about people, stop. If you are looking at pornography, quit looking. Get rid of those movies that have *any* pornography in them. If you are using the exploits that comes with money or prestige, turn from it and thank God for His blessing, and bless others. This will please God. It will also liberate your heart from greed and pride. These are powerful strongholds. God's ways are free to us. He wants us to give as freely as He does (see Matt. 10:8).

We train our senses to distinguish good from evil because our senses relate things to our understanding and change our heart, and that affects others. Change usually starts with what a person *says*. Therefore, when we speak honestly, it comes from our heart (see Matt. 12:34–37). The tongue is a mighty force, and none can tame it (see James 3:8). However, we can practice discernment before we speak or act. The mindset of the world has taught us to say such things as, "I could just die," or, "I could never do that!" But God's Word says that I'll live and not die and will declare the glory of God, and that I can do all things in Jesus Christ, who strengthens me. By saying words of truth *aloud*, we start to train our thoughts, and we can claim the inheritance that Jesus gave us! Our hearts are established by speaking words of truth, which bring life and power.

Each area of a person's life has its own dialect. The professional world teaches a different lingo than that used at home. We are educated, learning to talk the jargon of an area of expertise accepted in our part of the world. People of God must study and learn to talk the talk of the Kingdom of Heaven and not Christianese in every situation. We must learn to speak and see clearly the truth in each of these cultural settings. Words are powerful! They carry weight that affects the ones who use and hear them. Words hold a measure of esteem to the degree that a person has the wisdom to understand them and their use.

What we *see* is another matter, for people are visual beings. Therefore, everything flows in and out of the eye. The Scripture says that if the eye is good, the whole body will be good. The eye views the good and the bad. The eye is either light or darkness. Enlightening happens through the eyes—for the light of the eye is life, and if the eye is dark, how great is that darkness (see Matt. 6:22–23). Darkness is death because it is ignorance of God who is Light. It results in no light in a person's life shining out into the world. If we see ourselves as dumb, weak, and poor people, or if we see our children as never amounting to anything, or perhaps the opposite is true, and we think highly of ourselves because of intellect, wealth, or power, we need to recognize this type of thinking as the eye's view. Whatever we set our eyes on sways our opinions and brings or strengthens those good or bad thoughts that can develop into actions. Always remember to measure by God's perspective, viewing our children and ourselves as God's children who have eyes to see from another country. We must walk humbly in integrity with the Lord. God uses a higher standard than humankind. He views a person through the "Jesus lens"—with ruthless love and with actions of heroic proportions.

The eye is the light-bearer. One Easter season, in the *Imperial Valley Press*, there was a story of a new Believer in Jesus Christ. This Saint said that one of the things he noticed after becoming a Believer was how everything was so much prettier. The trees were greener, and the world was brighter and more colorful. When salvation comes, it chases away the darkness of the natural realm. The kingdom of this world is brighter in and around us when a person accepts Jesus.

Another sense is that of *hearing*. Have we heard condemnation so long that we say and think condemning thoughts? Do we hear guilt or make others feel guilty? The word "guilt" means to be held in by death. We understand this because sin makes all humankind guilty. Saints, we need to understand the magnitude of the words we hear and say. Remarks such as, "You're the smartest person in the world" or "You're so beautiful/ handsome" or "Everyone in our family dies young" or "You're dumber than dirt," are things we say without thinking. These words keep a weight of pride or fear or condemnation on us. By correcting these words, we can begin to change our mindset. To begin to change my words, I say, "I didn't mean that. Instead I mean, you're a new creation in Christ Jesus." Just because we have always used certain words, we don't have to continue. Stop, make a 180-degree turn, and hear what God says about the subject. Hear the good things God said. "For there is therefore now no condemnation for those who are in Christ Jesus" (Rom. 8:1). Now that we have read what Truth has said, what will each of us do with what we've heard? Choose today whom you will serve (see Josh. 24:15). Each day we choose to bow to God or to the ideas of the world. Hearing is an instrument of battle because it is bendable, as is written in Proverbs 22:17 (KJV), "Bow down thine ear, and hear the words of the wise, and apply thine heart unto my knowledge."

God set a standard. He knows about all the sounds in the world that attract us and call for our attention. God asks His followers to train their ears to hear and be sure of His Word in our heart. Some of the ways that Saints can correct negative speech is to listen and sing music that has words that are according to God's character. We should read books that encourage God's perspective. Be selective of TV, Internet, games, and anything that will affect our ability to hear God—because faith comes by hearing!

In Ezekiel 2, God instructs Ezekiel to go to Israel, saying they are a rebellious house. He was to speak God's Words to them. They should listen to you. In Ezekiel 3, he instructs, "Moreover, he said to me, 'Son of man, take into your heart all My words which I shall speak to you, and listen closely [with your ears].'" Our mouths and our ears are a vital part of our lives, not only in the physical, but also in the spiritual realm. We are to edify and encourage as we declare words to ourselves and to others.

Smell prepares our pallet for taste. The aroma of barbecued meat makes our mouth water as the aroma wafts to us. It increases our appetite. But what if the aroma emitted was more like the smell of fear—or bitterness? Do we smell like something that has begun to rot? On the other hand, does sweetness emanate from us? Can people smell the fragrant aromas of peace and well-being? The smell of good fruit is sweet all the way from the blossom to the last bite. Our aroma is a sweet fragrance in our lives ascending to the Father.

Prayers ascending to God give off a welcome aroma. This is an image of the burning incense rising to God from the Altar of Incense before the Holy of Holies. In *Smith's* page 265 regarding incense, "It would seem to be symbolical, not of prayer itself, but of that which makes prayer acceptable, the intercession of Christ." Jesus, our great High Priest, is interceding in the presence of the Father on our behalf. He is making our prayers acceptable.

Prayers can take on many aromas. We can emit desperation, anger, or joy as well as other emotions. Whether in prayer with our eyes open or shut, this pouring forth to God is an act of love. We find communion exciting as we experience an intimate relationship when talking matters over with an all-loving Father.

Taste and see that God is good. For God has given ruling words as in Proverbs 22:20–21, where He says, "Have I not written excellent sayings for you, sayings of counsel and knowledge, teaching you true and reliable words, so that you can give sound answers to him who sent you?" (paraphrased).

Through training our five physical senses, we acquire discernment in our lives. Taste produces understanding in us. It brings refinement. It flavors our judgment and reason. In *Hebrew* some of the meanings of *taste* include: "It diminishes or adds to a building of character, to give to be tasted; then by a common metaphor, in which taste is applied to understanding. What a person tastes, is to imbue them with anything, to instruct, to train up. As in Proverbs 22:6, 'Train up a child according to his way,' as to his manners and habits."

We need only to go after things God's way, with God's perspective not humankind's. When a person desires to have all things added to their life, it is imperative first to seek God's reign and His righteous standards. With the appetite to taste and see the goodness of God's ways, we mature in our understanding of Him. Our active participation in the affairs of His family heightens our adventure as we taste and digest the counsels of God's Word in our communion with Jesus on life's journey.

Then, we need to watch what we *touch*. Touching something adds our strength and agreement to the thing touched. It is the sense we use to perceive things by physical contact. What have we put our hand to? Is the work that we do honorable? Is it trustworthy or is it for unjust gain? Has greed led to stealing by touching someone else's property? Do we stand on the solid foundation of God's standards and ordinances or the mire of lies and deception? In our life do we stand on the shifting sand of decaying morals, bad character, and bad attitudes versus the solid foundation of righteousness, justice, and honor? To what have we added strength by participation? It might be a touch such as a mark made when supporting a concept or supporting a person when we vote.

Like Esau, our hunger may be more about our present needs—rudimentary things—than that which could be a future blessing that would mature us beyond the first principles. This blessing comes only by knowing God—wrestling with God to train our senses to submit to Him. Because Saints do not know the rules of the Land of Promise (rules not of this earth), the enemy takes their blessing away. We try to take our blessing back by acting and trusting in the laws and rules of the world. Haven't we learned yet that it does not work this way? To retake possession of the blessing, we need to keep the rules of Heaven. Then we will overrule the kingdom of this earth.

GUARDS

Training our senses gives understanding about guarding our gates—the gates of our heart, our life, and our eternity. These gates stand against the enemy and all his wily devices to abort, pervert, and devastate our family, state, and nation.

Becoming refined by our five senses narrows and guides us in a way that gives Saints an understanding of eating the flesh of Christ in communion. We get to know Him, and we can use that knowledge in life. When tasted and understood, the Holy Spirit descends and imbues, permeates, and influences us with power.

Through training, a person avoids bad consequences and enters a life of freedom by knowing boundaries. Boundaries have a starting point and an end for the good of the person. God's boundaries are for our good and are not for evil. They give us hope and a future, not a life filled with calamities (see Jer. 29:11). Boundaries begin at birth, and then each new area adds more. When we enter the door of salvation, we come to a new frontier. Boundaries, with regard to what is evil and good in God's view, help protect us—such as what God says about adversity and illness versus well-being and health. The Kingdom of Heaven has knowledge of everything we need that will set us apart from the upside-down wisdom in the kingdom of the world. Consecration is necessary to be sons and daughters of God. We are called to come out of where we were in our culture, our traditions, our worldview or mindset (see Psa. 45:10). Part of our perfecting (our sanctification for good works) is for our glory to learn and change within the boundaries of Heaven's realm.

Jesus has instructed us to be as little children. We are to thoroughly settle into the Father's family. He adds that unless we become as little children, we cannot easily enter the Kingdom of Heaven (see Luke 18:16–17). As children, we trust whatever our Father says. We are eager to do everything and to learn to do the things that are new to us. We practice to perfect what we have already heard, seen, touched, said, and tasted for ourselves by useful experience. And then, for the joy that is set before us, we look in anticipation for what God will be doing in our future.

> My heart is not proud, O LORD, my eyes are not haughty; I do not
> concern myself with great matters or things too wonderful for me. But
> I have stilled and quieted my soul; like a weaned child with its mother.
> —Psalm 131:1–2

Here David gives us a view of the necessary intimacy of his hope and reliance on God. David was a possessor of the promises in the Kingdom of God here on earth. Even as the renowned King of Israel, he still knew how to be a child with his Heavenly Father. Even when God disciplined him, David humbly submitted. As a man under the authority of God, David bowed to the boundaries of his Lord. Gladly outspoken in his regard for the Great *I AM*, King David never denied the respect entitled his Sovereign King. As people of God, we too need David's key qualities.

It's not the world that stands for God. Rather it is God's chosen and anointed who stand for Him.

David sought to understand the mind of His Lord, and he was unyielding to the persuasions of humankind. He held onto his trust in God alone. David could rest even when experiencing the demands required of a king. He knew the One who overthrows and establishes kings. After all, God had chosen and anointed a shepherd boy to be king, priest, and prophet. In the world's view, it was not likely that David could rise to such a status. In his writings, David fully conveyed the fact that what he had done was by the provision of Almighty God. Within the assignment and purpose of David's life, he had the ability to put into words those things not easily grasped by the mind of mortal man.   To acquire the "rest" that David describes takes effort. When we Christians do not turn to God's discipline or bow to the Lord's instruction, we allow our life, as well as our whole house, to be broken into. We allow treachery and evil to invade our domain as stated in Psalm 80:12–13: "Why have you broken down its walls so that all passing by pick its grapes? Boars from the forest ravage it and the creatures of the field feed on it."

When our walls, which are represented by the standards and boundaries of God's Word are broken down, the enemy (boar) comes in and beats us up. He *comes only to steal, and kill, and destroy* (see John 10:10). We have to be on our guard—to be alert to the attack of the enemy who shuts us up emotionally as well as physically. The enemy thrust us through with hurtful words and actions. When the walls and hedges are broken down or removed, the wild and unruly creatures of the field—those that are untaught in the ways of God's righteousness and justice—come in to destroy and kill. Believers permit the breaking down of the walls of our nation, our family, and our home when we permit the invasion of worldly ideas. We cannot live in this world and avoid wrong from knocking on our life's door and seeking entry to our minds. We must, however, choose whether to dwell on wrong thinking and letting it take root. We are not to be taken out of this world, but to be protected from the evil one (see John 17:15).

EARLY GUARDS

I came from a protected family environment. My parents were watchful and alert to any danger to their children, even from relatives. This applied to everyone. I had cousins who came to visit who would use bad language or be disrespectful. My earthly father would tell them something like this, "You will not use those words or do those things here. If you don't obey, you will have to go home. You're not welcome here if you do not live by our rules."

They always changed because they liked to be with us. To let them have their way would have influenced us children in a negative way. That is what happens when we let something stay in our mind or in our family that might influence us to turn from a right standing with the truth of God.

BOUNDARIES FOR LIFE

Our Book of Instructions sometimes seems harsh, but later we realize how wonderful the contents really are. It reveals the boundaries, lines of justice, and righteousness which have fallen in pleasant places (see Psa. 16:6).

If you have ever owned property, you know it had boundaries. Everything inside those boundaries was yours. If you prepared the land and worked at it diligently, then the land would produce good things. If you failed to prepare and care for the land, it would become desolate and produce weeds—things of no value. The reward for your labor far outweighed the sacrifice and energy it took to keep or clear the land.

THE NEED FOR DISCERNMENT

Every country's traditions include fun practices of celebrating holidays. People make great efforts to attend these celebrations. We think nothing of our traditions until events like September 11, 2001, happen when the world was shaken by terrorist attacks on America. Saints in America got serious in prayer, seeking God's help and protection. Many people sought some form of a higher power. Even national television discussed prayer. We got busy hanging flags, going to church, and putting up signs declaring "God Bless America." It is true that we need the blessing of God as never before.

Nevertheless, a couple months after being terrorized, many in this country celebrated Halloween, the eve of All Saints' Day. We did not recognize evil rising in our midst. So on October 31 we paid homage to the father of lies, the destroyer, who deserves no honor. Bowing to this enemy, we honored fear and death.

We have had this traditional holiday all our lives. Whitewashed with costumes and sweets, we teach our children to revel in it when it comes. We think it is just fun and is what everyone else is doing. Some adults even enjoy it above all holidays. Our children often rule over adults who think that love means letting them participate in ungodly things such as Halloween. However, love for our children constitutes telling them the truth about good and evil. We must train them to know the difference between wrong and right. Why would any parent allow a child to touch what wants to kill them? There is nothing wrong with dressing up or celebrating, but who and what are we celebrating? God has not given the enemy a day of honor or of celebration, but we have. Saints have failed to go against the culture in America by celebrating such days as Halloween. By touching in agreement with the holiday makes us partners in lifting it above what God says. Every day is the Lord's day! It is our responsibility to be loyal to Jesus our Lord over all other lords. God said that what we allow on earth will be allowed and what we do not allow will not be allowed, so stop allowing it. Christians can take the land back by changing whom we show forth in celebration and by not touching the unclean things.

This does not mean that we are to be afraid of touching or going places. They have no power over us until we bow to them. We must examine ourselves to see where our mindset is. Is it set in the Kingdom of God or in the kingdom of the enemy? Whose camp are we living in? When something wrong has a pull or tug on us, we need to stay completely away from it and not put ourselves in harm's way, for sin has pleasure for a season. Sin often looks and feels good, but later it is bitter. Darkness has no partnership with the way of light.

God's way is of light. In part, the meaning of "light" in the Hebrew has to do with purpose and knowledge. "Darkness" in Hebrew has to do with the ignorance of not knowing the wisdom of God. When we are confused about certain ideas of what is right or wrong, two minds exist. We are not of one mind. The solution is to get the Bible out and stay in the Scriptures to find the straight and narrow path of righteousness—God's way. It brings peace and rest. Confusion is not of God or His people. Let me repeat this again: The work of darkness has to do with the ignorance of not knowing God's Truth. God's light has to do with knowledge and understanding His way.

With the high price of His blood, Jesus purchased whomever will accept Him. Therefore, we are not our own, to do whatever we please (see 1 Cor. 6:19–20). Saints are to please the Almighty God, and by pleasing Him, we will be happy and fulfilled. Because what often pleases a person brings death, God knows what will benefit or damage us. By obeying His instructions about the limits to our boundaries, we can recognize what to allow in and out of our gates, and the result will be our contentment, for in righteousness is salvation, and in rest and peace is our strength (see Isa. 32:17).

Heroes of God treasure their time with the Holy Spirit. They depend on His instruction. They wait patiently for Him to supply their needs. They have a keen ear for the Counselor's voice, and He keeps them from the diverse evils in the world. With their senses trained, they enjoy solid food as those that are becoming mature/perfect in the Kingdom of God.

Discernment is a lifelong journey of training our senses to judge between right and wrong. Because the enemy is always using partial truths or twisting them, he perverts what is out in the marketplaces of life. He is busy trying to keep humankind marginalized and deaf to the Words of Life. Until we come to our senses, we, like the prodigal son, remain far from our rightful position with the Father in our Promised Land. The son in the pigpen (see Luke 15:17) recognized that the life he thought was so free and liberal, was really evil. Then, having come to the realization of what he had when he was living at home, he understood how good it was inside the boundaries of the dwelling place with his father and brother—no matter the friction in the family. He humbly and gladly turned to go back to the narrow place of clear vision, good taste, understanding, unconfused sounds, sweet aromas, and pleasant touch as he returned to a joyful and loving father.

> They will come to their senses and escape from the trap of the devil, who has taken them captive to do his will.
> —2 Timothy 2:26

- What basic principles of the Kingdom of God should I know?
- What are the boundaries of the Kingdom of Heaven?
- How will training my five senses in discernment guard my heart and life for eternity?

Chapter 8

DISTRACTIONS—
EYE STOPPERS

BELIEVERS STRUGGLE WITH many distractions in life while trying to live the life set apart. We struggle to conceive the impossible and the amazing. The sanctified life is hard to live when we are assaulted on every side at almost every moment by forces of the world. These worldviews attacks us through our eye-gate, capturing our mind. Deeming them worthy, we procure them whether they are good or evil. Therefore, we are to recognize them and judge them right or wrong in the perspective of the Realm of Heaven.

The perplexities of the ways we can easily be distracted are diverse. For instance, when I loaded up and took off to Bible college, vain imaginations of how to survive financially bombarded my mind. The extreme nagging in my mind with regard to my lack of income hampered my decisions. Perhaps more to the point, I could not trust God to support me. I had the fearful thought that maybe leaving my job was my idea and not God's. I finally took the leap of faith, and even though finances were a real struggle, God supplied.

Relying on God alone to meet my needs took violent faith. As I trusted God, He put me in various places beyond my expectations. For one, at college I intended to take counseling classes because I had done some successful counseling in the past. To my amazement, as I was led by the unseen influence of the Holy Spirit, I ended up with a couple of pastoral classes and several mission studies. I was challenged to trust God with my classes, and He continued to amaze me at what He had in store. Yielding to God is still a big battle for me because it means laying down what I see in life, picking up my execution stake (the cross), and following Jesus.

Following Jesus called for me to stop and prepare—to get my priorities right. First, I decided to weed out the unnecessary things that filled my time and to stop using my time for several secular media items, music, or just constantly being busy. I set aside more personal time with Jesus so that I could learn to see with my Heavenly Father's eyes! Learning to overcome distractions can start out simply. It doesn't have to be something big such as uprooting your whole life.

One of the snares the enemy places in our path is with business or "my ministry" and not God's. Well, God wants us to deny *ourselves* and follow Jesus who is the Truth; thus declaring our self untrue, coming away from what "we think" or "want to do." Instead of filling our lives with pursuits such as staying busy with a job, ministry, family, activities, and empowering self, we need to pursue the one necessary thing—to say Jesus is Truth. He is the One I will emulate. My occupation is in Him.

OVER-DESIRE

One of the meanings of lust in both the Hebrew and Greek language is, *over-desire*. In western civilization "business" and the "lust of the flesh" probably run neck and neck with the "over desire for money." These desires are not bad in themselves because money, flesh, and work are necessary. In *Webster's Dictionary*, "human life" is not a description for *business*. We live in the world, but it is the over-desires/lusts for the carnal that set us out of order. Saints have to guard against being *owned* by the desire to make money, being controlled by working all the time or against having the over-desires of the flesh. These tendencies are in each of our natures. The enemy is not a creator. He uses only what humankind allows him to use to keep us marginalized. Our lusts become the snares that catch and hang us in the air without a foothold on solid ground. Believers overload themselves with the things in life that we deem necessary. We think we can't relinquish any of them, but they detour us from the goal of Heaven and from seeing as God sees. "In the eye of the beholder," speaks of those things presented to our mind to look upon, to contemplate, then to discard or incorporate into our occupation and life.

Do not be confused by the clamor of the world and the monopolizing power of our culture's urgency to fill our senses with more and more materialism. Such things stop our view, leaving no room for the Kingdom of Heaven. In business or occupations of the world, no place of respect is given to what the world considers false words. That is, non-believers think God's Words are false. They only consider what they learn in the carnal realm as truth.

WHAT'S IMPORTANT?

The following examples in Scripture give us a view of staying on the narrow course. Amazing events thrust Elisha and Elijah together. Elijah had a directive from God to appoint another prophet (see 1 Kings 19:16 and following). Elisha is a man who has wealth and position—the big, important things in the eyes of humankind. That day Elisha's life was overturned when Elijah threw his mantle over him—a small thing, but an intense act. From that moment Elisha's life changed; he only asked to go tell his parents! Telling his parents was not a light thing. He was leaving his entire family and the wealth of the family business. He was leaving the place where his life was totally involved in the natural.

When Elijah found him, Elisha was plowing with twelve yoke of oxen. Was it twelve yokes, two oxen to each yoke? Was he driving the twelfth one? Elisha could have had servants side by side with yoked oxen plowing, as he oversaw their work. Whatever the case, he was among the wealthy of the land, for only the rich possessed so much. The land, equipment, the servants, and the oxen were his property.

The day was a sunny day with only a few wispy clouds on the horizon in the azure sky. What a beautiful day to be out in the open. Birds were singing and the air smelled earthy from the freshly turned ground. The sunlight shone off the turned mounds of dirt. There was the occasional snort of the oxen as they strained in the yokes on their necks. It was a great day to be alive! There was great satisfaction in a job well done. However, in the heart of Elisha was a longing—a longing for more, more of what valiant men do. He'd heard of historic men like Joshua and Gideon. He'd heard of the wonders of the Exodus out of Egypt. He knew the stories were true, because he lived here in Canaan among the historic places and stones of remembrance. Envisioning valiant acts of the past as he sits astride a chestnut steed, Elisha wants more—wants to be like the heroes of God.

Then came a big distraction! Elijah! Elijah approached and tossed his mantle over him. Elisha, mystified at first, thinks, *Why me? I am not a son of a prophet nor schooled as a prophet.*

Elisha values the call of God so highly that he killed all twenty-four oxen and had a barbecue to celebrate! The smoke ascended upward from the fire and the inviting smell of the meat roasting over a fire made from the wooden yokes tantalized the nostrils of everyone for acres. They all knew that something of importance was taking place—a covenant was being sealed by eating and drinking together. Twenty-four oxen will feed many people. Everyone in the area was invited to share in the celebration that announced Elisha's new start in the life-adventure of a handpicked child of God. Now, he would venture into areas he had never been before. Now, fearful of the unknown future, he would put vain imaginations behind him as he left his family.

Elisha totally turned away from his way of life, not to start a ministry of his own, but to become a mere student, humbly serving Elijah. Elijah was a daunting character. He called fire out of the sky that consumed legions of troops. He enjoyed making fun of the god of 450 false prophets of Baal! No one wanted to be around this austere madman. No one wanted to mess with the God of Elijah! Not kings and not other prophets of God!

Elisha had been a respected businessman who now had nothing. He had associated himself with someone whom even others in that social class wouldn't even live around. Elisha's not embarrassed by the fact that Elijah is treated like an audacious outcast. In his zeal to obey, Elisha takes nothing of the old life with him. This is a violent act against the unseen forces of his life as he grabs hold of his new life and casts off the old. He sacrifices the old things, those that are familiar and that have supplied abundance and meaning in his life. He offers them by fire as a sweet aroma to God. By the sacrifice of his lips, Elisha blesses the God of Heaven and tells his parents and others—he may never see them again. He cannot be their provider. He may never give them grandchildren who will carry on their generation to run the "business." Unexpected, God's timing has come, and he has been chosen. Elisha obeys! He trusts! He leaps!

CALLED OUT

Then there is the well-born Paul of Tarsus, a Jew from the tribe of Benjamin who is also a citizen of Rome. After a remarkable event in which he meets Jesus, he leaves his position of esteemed Pharisee and his employment of apprehending criminals against the Jewish nation. Paul goes into seclusion to limit his distractions (Gal. 1:17). He is constrained to get away with God to prepare for the called-out ministry of Heaven. He has a great deal to cope with as he battles his vain imaginations, education, and his status in social and political positions. Getting his eyes correctly fixed on the Kingdom of Heaven is mandatory. After *three years*, Paul, a man who had already memorized the Torah and the Prophets, was finally ready for ministry. He did not just jump out there to try to do the works of God. He needed to spend time in preparation. Paul then starts doing what Jesus did and is recognized in the natural and supernatural realms. The recognition of Believers comes from seeing as Jesus sees and doing what Jesus does. Without God's presence and power with us, Christians are just like other people.

DON'T HURRY

We need to separate ourselves from the distracting roar of the world so that we can study the Scriptures in quality time. Not hurrying, we can slowly mull over the Word of God. As we eat the Holy Scriptures, chewing on its words, meditating on every word for correct understanding, we are able to walk them out. God's Truth soaks in and our thoughts are renewed. Our being is filled. When lying down to rest, try to remember what the Scriptures you read that day said. Go to sleep thinking the thoughts of the Kingdom of Heaven. Let go of the turmoil in the world that screams for our attention. Try to comprehend how the events of everyday life relate to God's ideas. See how God shows Himself in each chapter in the way God deals with each person and the things He cares about (often the little things are the most important). So try to notice and study the little things. They will surprise you and often open your eyes to more understanding. People often say that their marriage or relationship went sour, not because of a major disaster, but that it was the "little things." Or that they fell in love because of the little things done in courtship. Little things are important.

OFFENDED BUT NOT DEFEATED

"Offense" in the Hebrew language means, "to mar or lame." Any offense or laming affects our walk in life. "Offenses will come, overlook them (see Prov. 19:11). Offenses will stop the eye, and if allowed to linger, will rob us of peace and further sight. By looking past the offense, we have restoration to wholeness because we do not struggle against human beings but against spiritual forces (see Heb. 16:12). When the enemy uses someone to come with offenses that injure us, it is a relief to know that the enemy is only using that person's words or deeds. Don't take it personally. Usually a person, doing the offense, either does not know or cannot do anything about it because of the sin nature in them. If the offense is not offending Jesus, then it should be easy to forgive. The first step to recovery is to recognize that it is really from the adversary. The second part is to forgive the person until the offense is gone—restoring the soul to peace. To recognize the tactics of the enemy, and not the person he uses enables us to extinguish all the flaming arrows, aimed at our heart, by the shield of faith (see Eph. 6:16). As faith increases, the enemy's relentless attacks change, and our stand must be vehement in faith against new tactics.

Heavily-laden offenses of words and deeds taint our freedom when we take them personally instead of giving them to Jesus. Do not take offense personally. Jesus said, offenses will come, but don't let any offense take hold. Forgive. Let it go! When an offense persists, tell the Father that you do not want to think on it. Ask Him to help you to forgive the offender, and ask him to take the offense from your mind. From experience, I know that He hears and will bring release.

Ever since the time of Jesus, there has been a spirit of rebellion at the mention of His name, which offends the carnal nature and angers many people. This is not strange, because the spirit of antichrist is in the world. It is a spirit that persuades humankind to hold the name of Jesus in disdain and rejection. His followers are hated for His name's sake (see John 15:18–25). This does not mean we should stop using the name of Jesus, but we should recognize there are those who do not love Him as much as they love the world.

In Bowing We Serve

Regard for someone is in the eye of the beholder. Therefore, Believers take care not to have less esteem for God than we do for ourselves or someone else. The Word of God is not a small thing. In fact, if we do not fear God more than we reverence humankind, then trouble crouches at our door. Will humankind mock God? He will not be treated as a person treats a child by listening to the child but then doing what that person desired to do all along. God is worthy of all honor and praise. He does not change, but because He is merciful, He waits for humankind to change. For the Word has life in it; without it, the wrath of God rests on the human race (see Eph. 2:3).

Often, Christians are distracted or caught up in whom to honor—even when attending a certain denomination becomes more important than the One we're there to glorify. Believers have included ideas from narrow doctrines of their denomination as to what God commands instead of elevating only Christ Jesus. Many continue to assemble in buildings long after the presence of God has left. These places are called "Ichabod," meaning "the glory has departed." Many Christians want to be known by the founder of the denomination who had the special revelation, or by the revelation making the name of a person heard more important than the name of Jesus. Oh, the enemy is sly and crafty. God's Word says that Jesus is the Spirit of prophecy (see Rev. 19:10). Paul reprimands the Saints in Corinth saying that he thanked God he had not baptized any of them except Crispus and Gaius and the household of Stephanas. This would prevent the Corinthian Saints from becoming followers of him more than followers of Jesus. The only baptism that counts is the one into Jesus. His baptism is the only one that will stand when God the Father comes to inspect His people (see 1 Cor. 1:10–17).

BAD HABITS

Bad habits are often hard to break. It takes persistence to get free from them. For instance, we hear the renown of the god of chance lifted up all the time. Humankind's seeking after luck gives it power over every area of life. Just try to stop saying "good luck." Notice how often even Christians say, "That was lucky," or, "Good luck with that." When did our God become a god of luck? If you know a Christian who speaks this way, and he or she will *not* listen to the truth of God, it may be necessary to stay away from that person. It is too easy to get distracted and start to agree by bowing in silence to the idol of luck.

The God of Truth reminds us repeatedly that if we, who call ourselves Believers, want luck to save us, then let the god of luck do it. The One True God is a God of blessing and cursing; truth and of life. He's One of certainty—the one we can count on. We need to start thinking of applying some brakes to the direction in which we are racing. Turn and face in the opposite direction, strive to gain that necessary intimate relationship with Jesus. Start saying, "I don't believe in luck or chance, but in blessing—surety." We are to redeem time, to buy it back. This does not leave the time we have to chance. Be certain.

When our eyes are stopped, distracted by humankind's ideas, we end up not taking God's Word as a reality, but speak despairingly of it. At times we depreciate the value of Jesus as we make Him seem small and do not esteem Him as God. He is, however, the exact expression of the Father. Other examples of this kind of language are: "You know God can't be bothered with little things like a headache or my sick cat." How about this one, "I don't know if God can forgive this or that?" "Well, that was then, now is now, and God doesn't do that anymore," when referring to such things as healing of body, emotions, and our soul. Or concerning the pouring-out of the Holy Spirit, some may say, "Well, they needed it then, we don't need it now. After all, we're educated." Well, education is not able to cure all things malignant, but God can.

We make God seem smaller by thinking that the devil has more power or that humans are all-powerful. Humans are so frail that sickness preys upon them and death overpowers them all. But Jesus defeated sickness, death, hell, and grave at the cross. So be careful. Treachery means to be without faith in the God of Heaven, so a Christian without faith in God is carnal and not able to please God. Do we understand faith? Trust is complete confidence in leaning on Jesus, becoming one of the faithful remnants of the great crowd spoken of in Hebrews, chapter eleven. These people had faith, complete trust in what God can do. Many times, as we read their stories of faith, it seemed that at times they had none. But trust grows, and in the end, God counts them as faithful. *God, forgive my slight regard for You and my underestimation of You and what You do every day. For every day declares the wonders You alone have created.*

UPSIDE-DOWN VIEWS

The love of Christ crosses all boundaries and every nation. However, the world views others by skin color, eye color, hair, gender, or age. This view stops the eye to determine how attractive the object is. It limits the esteem of the beholder. But God is not a respecter of persons. He looks at the heart, not the outside of a person. It is the heart that is judged by God and not the appearance. There is neither Jew nor Greek—circumcised or uncircumcised are alike (see Col. 3:11). Because God so loved the world that He gave His only begotten Son, that *whosoever* will open his or her heart and come, will be saved (see John 3:16).

God created color, gender, and beauty, and He shows no favoritism even with age. If what Saints see stops them, they are babes in the Kingdom. God does not take sides. He is interested only in the inside of a person. The valiant of God are interested in the same things. There are no politics with the God of Truth, for He is always correct, just, and merciful. Though He had, and has, many people in the political arena, they must line up with His Word.

POWER UNKNOWN TO US

Because eye stoppers keep our view in the wrong places, God's people live a subnormal life in the kingdom of the world. One of John G. Lake's books ends with a phrase that really caught my attention. It said that when the demons see a Christian, they say we have power *but we don't know it!* This incredible truth has not been included in most Christians' education. Saints have power, but they don't know it! Let us know the Father intimately so our mind is set on the ways of His Kingdom. Let's be out of our own mindset and have the mindset of Christ with our Father's eyes.

Fear is a low-ranking officer in the kingdom of the enemy (see Isa. 36:9). It crouches before each of us, and at the first sign of acceptance springs, capturing us. In the spiritual realm, fear comes against us first. By our first response we can win the struggle. Isaiah 36–37 (paraphrased) gives the battle instructions. When fear comes, *don't listen!* Do not speak to the spirit of fear, *but CRY OUT to God,* who will save and strengthen us. Do not be afraid. Drive fear away by knowing what the Lord has said; trust the Lord and He will come and save us. We have more power to overcome than we realize.

Certain of what we hope for and certain of what we do not see, the power that Saints possess lies hidden in the realm of our trust and combats what we perceive in the kingdom of the world. Fear and ignorance keep our viewpoint of the supernatural at a distance. This keeps Christians at a disadvantage because humankind travels in a way that is opposed to God. Fear is eager to control us. Captured by all kinds of fears that keep us from being bold and courageous in this world, we are forced off the straight and narrow. The unseen forces of fear keep us from accomplishing what Almighty God plans for us. The fear of death captured Cain as he pleaded with God to protect him (see Gen. 4:14). And it was fear that kept Adam and Eve hiding from their closest Friend, God. Fear will also keep us from the smallest gesture of reaching out. There are simple ways to break fear's grip, as told in the following story:

One fall day as I was leaving lunch, I walked down the street toward work. I looked at the wonderful colors of leaves on the trees. The air was crisp, but not too cold yet. A young man started to pass me and said, "Hi, I like your jacket."

Responding I said, "Thank you, have a nice day."

As he passed, he answered, saying this is the best part of the year, and to have a nice day. He was dressed in a black leather jacket and dark pants. His dark hair had a curl to it. He looked harmless enough, but fear of any further conversation came immediately to my mind. At the same time, I did not want to miss the opportunity I felt the Holy Spirit was giving me. I quietly said, "Not too hot, cold, and beautiful colors, and spring is like that too."

He slowed down a bit to let me catch up, and in a lower discouraged tone said, "Makes you wonder why we keep going under?"

Now, even more hesitant, but in order to offer him hope, I said, "Well, we don't have to. If you know God; you won't go under. God bless you."

Now, still walking and turning slightly to face me, he smiled and responded, "And you. I'll take that blessing, I felt it."

He now slowed down completely so we could stroll along together. Trying to inspire him, I said, "We should encourage and bless each other."

He stuck his hand out as I did mine. Grasping hands, we both said, "God bless."

As we traveled on, he remarked, "You know, I don't know why I wasn't bold?"

Encouraging him I answered, "The enemy keeps us in fear, to shut us up and to say nothing."

The young man opened up, confessing, "Wasn't that way when I was a kid—talked about God. No lying, no cheating—now . . ." His voice trailed off, "I'll change," his tone was now promising.

As we came to the corner and the parting of our ways, I asked him if he had a Bible. He assured me that he did. Smiling and shaking hands we parted with a last "God bless."

Fear is not to have dominion over us. It is not to stop us from any opportunity to reach out and draw a person closer to the Kingdom of Heaven. Though there is a mighty crowd of the lost around us, our job is just to talk to the one God places in our path. We are to keep our eyes on Jesus as God shows us favor. "To enjoy His favor" is an image taken from the custom of kings, who only admitted into their presence those whom they favored. God provides strength to vanquish the darkness. To the amount that Jesus lives in us, we as Christians bring the Kingdom of God near people. No words or deeds go unnoticed or wasted, for God sees and will honor any gesture done to glorify His name.

Were not the Cushites and Libyans a mighty army with great numbers of chariots and horsemen? Yet when you relied on the LORD, he delivered them into your hand. For the eyes of the LORD range throughout the earth to strengthen those whose hearts are fully committed to him.

—2 Chronicles. 16:8–9

- What worldly things have my eyes stopped on?
- God has called us to a humble life. How am I serving?
- How can I stop taking offenses personally?
- The Holy Spirit has given me power for Kingdom life. How am I using it?

Chapter 9

ALL THAT IS
REQUIRED OF ME

IN MARK 9:23, JESUS said, "Everything is possible for one who believes." It is a simple statement, but one that is hard for Christians to fully comprehend. To be persuaded to live our life as the faithful are called to do, we are to believe that God is and that He rewards those who earnestly seek Him (see Heb. 11:6). The requirement seems to be quite simple. Just believe God. Well, how many of us have tried this? We say, "I believe God," and then circumstances get in the way.

Believing is a cornerstone of the Christian life and is what marks the faithful in the Bible. Abraham believed God, and it was counted to his righteousness, and God calls him friend (see Isa. 41:8; Jas. 2:23). When God recognizes a person, it is because they believe and obey Him; they are no longer submissive to the standards of the world. Honor and loyalty come with friendship, and where there is belief in someone or something, an alliance is formed. James 4:4 states that friendship with the world is adultery and hatred toward God, and that *anyone who chooses to be a friend of the world becomes an enemy of God.*

In the Greek language, *belief* means, "to win over, a firm persuasion, conviction, faith, and belief in the truth . . . . Not the outcome of imagination but based on fact, such as the reality of the resurrection of Christ (1 Corinthians 15), and, as such, becomes the basis of realistic hope. And in 2 Corinthians 5:7 it says, "For we walk by faith, not by sight" meaning that which appears before us may not be what it seems to be, while faith . . . stands on proof."

"Stands on proof." What a strange thing to comprehend. Faith is being sure of what we hope for and certain of what we do not see (Heb. 11:1). Faith is completely foreign to "seeing is believing," a standard that is resident in our lives. We have lived our life only recognizing what we exercise by our five senses, usually without having a thought of the invisible. The spiritual world has been there all the time but lacked the concrete evidence needed to make us believe it is real. Yet, as we come into the family of God, we are to throw all our past away and view the unseen world as more real, more sure, and more alive than the natural world. Having our minds transformed, we are to be in the world but not part of the thinking and actions of this world system.

In Hebrew, the word "*belief*" means "to sustain, to support . . . . It is to stand firm, still, unshaken, and such as one may safely lean on. Metaphor, to be faithful, or to be trustworthy, . . . of a servant, . . . a witness . . . of God. It also means a man of approved wisdom. It means to be sure, certain, to be found true, confirmed."

It is clear to see why Jesus, as the faithful witness, stands firm in believing His Father in Heaven. Jesus speaks words that hold the full measure of certainty. Jesus, tried and tested, proved He stood for the truth of God. He spoke only the words of His Heavenly Father and did only His works. By the weight in their actions and words, Saints are recognized, for they know the guarantee that backs them. Wisdom is gained from times of trial and testing. We are tested and tried in the small things until we prove ourselves trustworthy in them. Then harder tests come to increase our faith, until we grow into maturity to the full measure of faith.

Without belief, there is no obedience. This seldom-examined element needs to be grasped and the principles understood of not being a hearer only, but becoming a doer of the Word. Jesus asked, "Why do you call me, 'Lord, Lord,' and do not do what I say?" (Luke 6:46), for if we are not going to obey what God says, why should we have the honor of calling Him Lord. In *Webster's,* the meaning of "obedient" implies "willing submission to control." Today we deem it almost barbarian to acquiesce willingly to a lord in the world. Instead, we teach taking control, empowering ourselves, and doing what feels good, which is opposite of denying self and taking up our cross to follow Jesus (see Matt. 16:24).

There are qualifications that insure us a place with the honorable. These qualifications distinguish those that are clothed with the garment of obedience. Christians are to be dressed in integrity of right standards, unselfish acts, and decorated with love and mercy. Integrity comes out of obedience. A righteous person's mouth utters words that are true and certain. He displays actions that resonate with compassion and self-denial. Heroes stand on God's Word and are never swayed no matter the cost.

Dressed in battle garments, and doing all, they continue to stand firm (see Eph. 6:10–18). By obedience, Believers show to whom they belong. They willingly serve others and bow humbly before the Lord who gives them recognition.

DELAYED OBEDIENCE

Several years ago, while I was working at my desk, the manager came in and asked the supervisor to do something. Immediately the supervisor, who was busy, stopped and jumped up to do what the manager wanted. I thought, *Wow, he just dropped everything to do what the manager said.* Instantly the Holy Spirit said to me, "I wish you'd do that for me." Oh my! My heart sank. I never stop what I'm doing immediately I usually think that I'll do it as soon as I get to a good place to stop. Now it occurs to me that delayed obedience is disobedience. Change had to come to my life. Old habits of self-service had to be broken.

TO OBEY IS BETTER

Whether we realize it or not, there is a battle going on, Saints. The battle rages daily in the supernatural for the souls of humankind. In submission, we render our decision to follow Jesus and to promote that which affects the natural. Saints share in the outcome by obedience in the battle.

A modern-day hero learned one of his greatest lessons from failure. As the missionary David Hogan stood over the drowned boy he had just pulled from the swirling floodwater, the Holy Spirit spoke to him. "Pray for him and I will raise him up." However, because of the crowd standing around and the cries of the parents, fear struck and overcame Hogan and he disobeyed. The enemy won that time. The missionary now understands that he is a *loser* if he is not obedient to Jesus! Today, signs and wonders follow this man.

Failure is not a stranger to any of us. We all fail. We learn not to make the same mistake twice. Well, sometimes it takes failing more than twice to learn what we need to know. Nonetheless, God is faithful, and as we yield to Him, He will complete the good work that He has started in each of us.

Obedience lacks a place of honor in society today. Our fear of failure and ridicule keeps us in the old ways of disobedience, leaving our thoughts held in the kingdom of this world. Fear keeps us in rebellion, which is as the sin of witchcraft (see 1 Sam. 15:23). The Bible says "to obey is better than sacrifice" (1 Sam. 15:22). In disobedience, we injure ourselves by doing what God hates. King Saul became a loser because of the people standing around him. His disobedience took him out of his kingly position with God. Samuel, in obedience, killed everything that Saul wanted to offer to God and did not worry about pleasing humankind, but the Almighty Potentate (see 1 Tim. 6:15 KJV). Saul lost everything while Samuel remained steadfast in the Kingdom of Heaven and retained his friendship with God. Is our heart like Saul's or is it like Samuel's?

Hebrews, once they heard what God had to say—usually from reading of Scriptures—bowed in obedience. They immediately incorporated God's instruction into daily life and by doing so lived their faith. They did not place either loyalty to friend or esteem to another above the honor given the great *I AM*.

Procrastination is not an option for the active participant in Heaven's reign on earth. Not once a week; not when we feel like it; not someday, but every day, real leaders make obedience a lifestyle. They seize the moment as soon as the Holy Spirit speaks. Obey, or lose the opportunity to walk with God and change history! God calls all Christians to be leaders to the measure of talent that He gives each of us (see Matt. 25:15–46).

The possession of a firm faith channels actions that will defeat the enemy. Doubt produces nothing. Trust in God establishes leaders who do not lean on their own understanding of the situation. Believers who have knowledge and confidence in Heaven's instructions are obedient. They know where their alliance belongs. It is paramount that the true Christian fears God (see Prov. 14:2). To fear is to go trembling in service. It moves us to obey, and without obedience, we experience ruin and destruction.

God will have His business done on earth, and the privilege of sharing authority with Jesus is our choice. It is the right of inheritance obtained by obedience. Our employment is not of this world, but it is to work at the King's business. True leaders value God, for they know Him. They *exert themselves in obedience*. A prince with God knows it requires quick action to defeat the enemy by ruining his tactics.

Lukewarm Saints are at a disadvantage. They are living in danger and in unbelief. The community in Ephesians lost their first love. If their love was not regained, the result would be the removal of their lampstand (see Rev. 2:1–5). When lukewarm Saints exert themselves, heat starts to radiate as they make every effort to move God-ward. They demonstrate passion that demands the cost of something valued. For example, time and energy are elements that are dear to us. To deny self and come away with the One who loves us is worth our time and energy. This price, willingly paid, ignites passion that retains our position with the King above all kings.

When we are recognized as Christians, we may lose friends, family, and perhaps a job or position. In other countries, the cost could be as high as the loss of life. Believing in Jesus costs something. Are we up to the challenge?

Old Testament Hebrew addresses the meaning of "obey" and "obedience" very nicely and covers the Greek as well. In Hebrew, these words mean, "to breathe after, hence to be inclined, to wish, to be willing in mind. In the negative it means to refuse, to loathe, turning away from and stagnant."

Therefore, we see that heroes through the ages have willing minds. They breathe after God. When Christians desire to follow God, a right standing with Heaven exists. When we are not willing to understand God's Word, it is unbelief, and we have no access to miraculous power.

Obedience and belief connect in the Hebrew. "Believing is also the meaning of hearing as opposed to seeing. Psalm 18:44 says, "As soon as they hear me, they obey me." As soon as they hear my mandate, they obey. To obey means to be sharp, acute . . . like sharp weapons—hence to listen, hear, obey, have an understanding heart, and a faithful witness, as opposed to a false one. It also means to utter a voice, especially to sing, to announce, especially those of female singers." In other places, the word "female" refers to those followers, who, like the evangelist, sing out the good news like the Bride of Christ.

There is no obedience without hearing and understanding in our heart, and there is no believing without obeying, and without obeying, there is no faith. In Hebrew 11:6 it says, "And without faith it is impossible to please God, because anyone who comes to him must believe that he exists and that he rewards those who earnestly seek him." This verse contains covenant language from our covenant-keeping God. As we unite in covenant (something thoroughly set down with Him), we form a team that gives us an opportunity to trust what God says He will do. God is not to line up with us. Rather we are to line up with Him. God is Sovereign. If God's Kingdom is first in our life, then He will supply everything we need. Saints are to be bold, strong, and sure, with a steadfast mind, daring enough to believe the Word of God over the words and traditions of the world, and to do all these things from God's perspective. This will perfect our strength.

Saints waste a lot of time doing things with no eternal value such as expressing unimportant thoughts, words, and doing what is not godly. In Micah 6, Believers have key elements of instruction; those of doing justice, loving-kindness, and walking humbly with God. Christians store up treasures in Heaven using these simple principles that surpass the knowledge of carnal thinking, and which are only accomplished when yielding to God's authority in our life.

By wisely spending time and energy in these areas, change will occur. "With what shall I come before the Lord and bow myself before the God on high? . . . He has told you, O man, what is good; what does the Lord require of you but to do justice, to love kindness, and to walk humbly with your God?" (Micah 6:6–8 NASB).

These requirements challenge Saints to know and understand *God's character*. Serving under the authority of God on High, they understand true justice from God's perspective. Real kindness from His view is not the same view as humankind's. By humbly walking in intimate union with God, we come into the King's Chamber (see Song of Solomon 1:4). There we come to know and serve our Bridegroom, our Lover.

To "do justice" is to do God's righteous and just ways rather than those of humanity. It is looking at real motives—those of the heart and not outward circumstances. God's justice is to love your enemies and pray for those who persecute you (see Matt. 5:44). Maybe you feel attacked by a fellow employee who took the sales commission that would give you enough to pay your bills. Perhaps you suffered further persecution when that same person threw it in your face, saying how great he had done this month. On the other hand, did someone tell your boss that they do all the work and that you are lazy?

Justice speaks up even when it hurts. Justice is also when we take time to care for widows who are fighting for their homes against tricksters who steal money, houses, children, and their good names. We are to care for orphans by making sure they have shelter, food, and provisions. We are also to test for accurate weights of judgments by knowing God's just and right standards keeping the scales of justice pure, not weighed with bribes for unjust decisions made by rules and words of humanity, which affect our lives through the justice system.

The just guard against those who gossip or spread malicious rumors. Those who commit murder with their mouth are like men lying in wait to destroy others. There is much to glean from our Book of Instruction while we fast, pray, and worship. Concerning all things, the just live by trusting what comes from hearing the Word of God. They listen and keep listening for God to reveal His mysteries. They love the Words of Life.

To love kindness is to show mercy when others do not deserve it. We are to love being kind just as God loves to be kind. He showed goodness when Jesus was crucified. Our mindset is to be the same as God's, who cheerfully gives precious grace equally to all (see John 1:16). Made in His image, Saints are meant to have constant and abiding favor. We need to have this love of kindness dwelling richly within us from our head to toes—knowing that mercies are securely promised to us. We can give love and kindness to others in the world.

God's love never quits, and His kindness endures for eternity. It is to our honor to be as glorious as He is. God is love (see 1 John 4:7–8). It radiates from Him like a consuming fire.

When Jesus fed the thousands, shortly after John the Baptist was beheaded, it was because Jesus loved kindness and put it before His own needs and feelings. Jesus must have felt awful grief when John, His natural cousin and closest spiritual brother, was unjustly murdered. Jesus was already tired, and yet people who needed attention continued to follow him. The day was warm there on the western side of the Sea of Galilee. A slight breeze rippled through the grass and leaves and ascended the slope to the place where Jesus and the disciples were. The breeze soothed the weary flesh, but the news of John's beheading was a lead weight on Jesus' heart. It had been a long, trying day, and Jesus knew that John would not be one of those He would raise from the dead. He had fed the crowd spiritually, and now, not wanting to send the people away without physical nourishment, He asks the disciples to have the crowd sit down. He will reveal to them who *God* is at all times—even in a tragic loss. Nothing will keep Jesus from being obedient and showing loving kindness to the thousands who came to learn and get help.

To "walk humbly with God" means knowing that our strength comes from God and not from ourselves. God desires a humble and contrite heart, not one that is rebellious or arrogant (see Psa. 51:17; Isa. 57:15; 66:2), not building up our own worth through intelligence, wealth, and strength, but through knowing and understanding the Lord, who exercises kindness, justice, and righteousness on the earth (see Jer. 9:23–24). Moses was known as the humblest of men. Yet, in the eyes of humankind, he was highly esteemed. Moses spent forty years just finding out that he was a mere man before God could use him. In the practice of his new calling, he learned that if God's presence did not go with him, he was nothing more than any other person. He was no more than grass, and neither are Believers. The One True God is not like any other god or anything else. We are to imitate His qualities—such as knowing His straight path and keen wisdom and His almighty power and wonder. Heaven is God's throne, and the earth is His footstool (see Isa. 66:1; Acts 7:49). Frail and weak humans are here today and gone tomorrow. Nevertheless, on earth, those who know their God do great things. We can walk with God like Moses and Enoch. To be a Moses or a David, much is required of us. We are to love and serve only the Living God.

The valiant Saints of God are the humblest of people. They do not brag about what they have done, but what Jesus does. They set their mind to obey completely, unyielding as they lay down their lives—even when they face physical death. In the image of God, they love to be kind and just to all, even to murderers, the outcast, the nasty, ugly, or smelly. No matter humankind's haughtiness or the wickedness of their heart, no matter if they are rich or famous, Christians are required to love the unlovely, for Jesus first loved us. Justice is on the lips of the courageous, and from their mouth words strike against darkness. They give all for God's Kingdom. They believe, obey, and trust God in all circumstances. They are unyielding! They work out their salvation with fear and trembling (see Phil. 2:12). They understand security in Jesus and that, "He became the source of eternal salvation for all who obey Him" (Heb. 5:9).

- Believing in things not seen, how have I stood on proof?
- Do my beliefs and obedience deserve God's trust in me?
- How have I loved being kind as God does?
- I have failed in the past. In which ways am I learning from them?
- Everything in life costs. Am I willing to spend my life for Christ?

Chapter 10

A SLAVE MENTALITY BLURS ABSOLUTES

LACK OF HEAVENLY glory nails our feet to the ground, enslaving us to the world's reign. Our eyes see only the visible, and we are unable to soar to new highs with God. We are unable to see beyond ourselves. The spirit of seduction immerses us into the enemy's counterfeit kingdom—into the slime pit of confusion. Knowledge and understanding of perverse traditional worldviews cause us to believe a "thing" must be true because we have always done the "thing" this way. It does not matter whether a person is wealthy, poor, or in between, or of various ethnicities or nationalities. Sin has infected every human being (see Rom. 3:23) and upside-down precepts influenced each one to live a perverse lifestyle. It sets the direction of the mind on the road to corrupt justice and impure morals and continually drags us to destruction as we sink in the quicksand of death.

What Jesus demonstrated clarifies blurred lines and gives the beloved spiritual eyes and supernatural powers to defeat the works of the enemy. To bring down the strongholds of worldly views is a battle with the soul and flesh that lifts the person from glory to glory, as they view the King of Glory.

In today's culture, where evil is called good and good is declared evil, little of God's standards are visible. Today God's absolutes of right and wrong are either not accepted or are so blurred that people have a hard time knowing where the line is (see Heb. 12:1). The mindset is, "I'm all right with who I am." Only when we define truth and error, good and bad, can humankind make value judgments. What someone defines as integrity, credibility, and goodwill, may be to someone else entirely different, and perhaps completely wrong in God's perspective.

For example, in Africa, a tribe's worldview of truth was to take other tribes' cattle when the cattle were left out after dark. The tribes that border on this tribe's land were not pleased with that concept of truth. Just because someone decides that, "It's not sin," does not make such a statement God's Truth.

Because all we know is the splendor of the many kingdoms of the world, they ensnare humankind in prison cells and death traps that blur the just and right boundaries of God's views. Truth, for Christians, rests in values and reasoning that are not of this world. Truth is set on God's standards and ordinances. As we strive to find out how and what the One True God values and thinks, we must use God's measure and weights of right and wrong as our *only* guide and standard.

At times, the unseen force of the Spirit of Truth engages us in a great wrestling with our disbelief and upside-down thinking. As we struggle with "What is truth?" we Believers must look to Jesus who is Truth and who came to testify of the truth (see John 18:37–38). There is not the slightest shadow of turning in Him. We do not have a wishy-washy God. He is straight in every way and abundant in His care for us. In the wrestling, we bend or break in acceptance or rejection of God's standards.

Moses was willing to step out of everything he knew and step into a strange culture. Turning his mind to understand the Most High God, Whom neither he nor his father knew, Moses was willing to stay in obedience to lead a murmuring people out of slavery. The way was obscure, but his obedience was absolute.

Jesus also stepped out of everything He knew and came to an upside-down world. Raised within the confines of Judaism, He displayed the wisdom of God and gained favor with God and man (see Luke 2:52). He never wavered in His obedience to His objective to purchase humankind back for His Father. As He desired to live life on display, so we his followers should desire to live the same life. Jesus is the Way, the Truth, and the Life (see John 14:6). Jesus supplies the power that liberates us from a life of drudgery, and He feeds us with real substance on the bread and wine from Heaven that allows Saints to soar! Escaping the gravitational hold of the world, we lift up above the horizon and go where sinful humankind cannot.

UNSEEN FORCES

With the pressures to be tolerant of all faiths smudging our vision, humankind believes that God tolerates the corruption of the world. God is not tolerant! God is longsuffering! God is timeless (eternal) giving opportunity for humankind to change (see 2 Pet. 3:9). Humankind is locked in time and thinks that God is all right with corruption just because wickedness has continued for eons. This thinking is erroneous. Darkness holds our understanding and necessitates a spiritual eye salve for seeing clearly. Sin is death, so why will God be okay with it?

One of the absolutes we find is that to have eternal life in Heaven, all human beings must be saved by the name of Jesus (see Acts 4:12). Tolerance says that Jesus is only one of the ways to Heaven. Those who believe this are secured in a stronghold of confusion that ends in hell. These counterfeits woo humankind to believe that whatever each man thinks is correct. The Kingdom of God is absolute. Life in this flesh is temporal, and we are to think past the present cosmos.

The onslaught of these unseen forces often infiltrates our mind in an overwhelming torrent to flood our reasoning and make the truth and righteousness of God indistinct. They smudge the clear and simple plan of salvation. They confuse our journey in the Kingdom of Heaven. God has only one plan to redeem all creation, Jesus. By the power of Jesus being lifted up for humankind to view, all will be drawn to Him (see John 12:32). God's plan is absolute, and every Christian needs to tell it as part of our witness and confession. This liberty of righteousness, truth, love, grace, and mercy are correct directions in the Kingdom of God. We need to obtain understanding and knowledge from God's vista.

When Jesus in Matthew 12:48, says, "Who is my mother, and who are my brothers?" he ask a confusing question of the audience who knows His natural parents—or at least they know they are waiting outside and are asking to see Him. In the verses immediately following, Jesus explains that His family consists of people who come out of the kingdom of darkness into the Kingdom of Light and those who come from blurred vision and confusion toward certainty and clarity. The beloved's eyesight improves with continuous reading of the Bible and seeing clearly its instructions. With loving kindness, the Holy Spirit provides eye salve for the healing of our wounds and the curing of our vision, enlightening our soul.

The cares of the world, stress, and sickness dim our view of God. Other impairments come from visual things like television that make it hard to spend time with Jesus and to get a view of the heavenly. Stress rates as one of the top killers of humankind. Pressures from unseen forces and the weight of keeping up appearances, offenses, and the quest for fortune weigh heavily on humanity. These cares keep our eyes fixed on the world's corrupt morals, bad character, and all types of perversion. *Greek* [worldly] standards constantly assail our minds, enslaving Christians to mix the ideas of the world and Heaven so that they look like everyone else! By these blurred ideas, many Christians are tasteless and tarnished, rather than light and salt. Instead of radiating pure light that pushes back darkness, Saints walk in a haze. Instead of having wonderful distinct flavors to give the hungry world so that they can know that God is good, Believers are stale and repel those who come near. Lost humanity has no desire to change their lives to follow Christ. They are unable to recognize Christians as different.

With the increase of knowledge, technology, and modern conveniences, humankind has faith in their self. The world's rhetoric and the spectacular things done by humankind blur our vision and dull our hearing. Trusting in the ability of humans, we settle for extreme confidence in the power of the god of mammon, intellectualism, humanitarianism, and scientific progress. Most western Christians surrender to the slavery of greed and are steeped in disbelief.

With all the voices in the world wooing humankind, the fear of going to hell is muted. People do not think Heaven or hell exist. And if there is a God, He is surely a God of love and too good to send anyone to hell. He will allow all to enter Heaven, no matter what. Some reason that living on earth is hell enough for anyone. Humankind's enslavement has stultified the fear of the Lord and taken all fear of God's judgment from humankind's thoughts. It is true that God is love and He is good. However, He is also absolutely righteous and just. "The fear of the Lord is the beginning of wisdom and knowledge of the Holy One is understanding" (Prov. 9:10). It is absolutely important that Christians seek out only God's supreme wisdom (see Prov. 4:7). It is necessary to fear the One True God in order to stand with Jesus. Otherwise, we bow to everything we meet. Within the Bible there are "first" things for us to do. These foundations are so important, for when we start to understand wisdom, it states that the first thing is to fear God. Until that is achieved, the rest of what our instruction says remains weakened and not readily understood. Many truths are blurred and mired in worldly thoughts, such as ideals and media images that stir our mind and put humankind on a pedestal above God. In Genesis 3, the serpent entices Adam and Eve. Here in the Hebrew words, Eve tells God, the enemy "lifted me up." We too need to examine ourselves to find anything lifted up above Jesus. Lifting up anything above Jesus brings ruin. Jesus tells us whom to fear in Luke 12:4–5:

I tell you, my friends, do not be afraid of those who kill the body and after that can do no more. But I will show you whom you should fear: Fear Him who, after the killing of the body, has power to throw you into hell. Yes, I tell you, fear Him.

Humankind's view of truth does not make the fear of God and His judgment null and void just because we do not recognize God or His Truth. Judgment is true because God is truth and cannot lie. He has said that it is appointed once for every person to die and then to face judgment (see Heb. 9:27). Judgment belongs to Jesus. God has given it over to Him (see Rom. 2:16). The wisdom of holy fear keeps our eyes on Jesus.

Jesus procured sinful humans for a price. His death on the execution stake/cross gave humankind an opportunity to change and go to Heaven instead of to hell. Jesus comes as the sacrificial Lamb. He rises from the dead as the Lion of the tribe of Judah. As the slain Lamb saves us, we start the journey in the Kingdom of Heaven. The Lion represents the King with a voice that roars and conquers all others. Therefore, we, who call Jesus Lord, need to bow and serve the King of all kings.

In Mark 7:13 Jesus declares that tradition renders the Word of God powerless because teaching traditions of humankind over the principles of God limited power to what only humans can do. Then absolute destruction ensues instead of knowing the Truth that sets them free to go beyond traditions.

The definition of sin is not within families or within nations. The God of Truth defined sin and measured it against Truth. He set the boundaries that judge sin. We are to express God's Truth in the various areas of life in every situation, no matter the claims of humankind's knowledge and expertise.

Many Saints have the slave mentality of formulas, self-will, determination, positive attitude, and more me-isms. Many of us, in the effort to be free from oppression, find that it is not so easy to leave the familiarity of this world. We cry out to be released but make no movement toward extracting ourselves from slavery's grip. When we are recognized in the spiritual realm, we seize the truth that humankind's way is not the way of the Almighty God as paraphrased here from Isaiah 55:8–9. "My thoughts," says the Lord, "are not like yours, and my ways are different from yours. As high as the heavens are above the earth, so high are my ways and thoughts above yours."

God's way is perfect in itself and is high above anything we can imagine. These ways define the lines for building on a solid foundation and erecting walls to keep us separate from the world. Those who are faithful stand tall in the certainty of these right and just ways. They are strong on God's absolutes (see Prov. 4:20–22). Even though we have never gone this way before, obedience is still an absolute requirement. We can obey in Jesus' name. God lovingly invites each of us to talk everything over with Him. He has made it possible to put off the shackles that tie our feet to this earth, freeing us to soar to new heights.

- What things have blurred God's Truth in my life?
- Is what God says a lie, partial lie, or all truth?
- How has the knowledge of Heaven and hell changed my desire to step out of carnal thinking?

Chapter 11

RELEVANT TO WHAT?

WHAT EACH OF us values, we hide in our treasure chest. These gems relate to personal feelings or opinions influenced by emotion or prejudice. Our choices portray what we recognize as truth relevant to our life. This is related to the hardness of our heart by the deceitfulness of sin (see Heb. 3:13). The darkness of sin exerts its power over us, but once we are rescued by Jesus, our lifestyle is supposed to change.

> So I tell you this, and insist on it in the Lord, that you must no longer live as the Gentiles do, in the futility of their thinking. They are darkened in their understanding and separated from the life of God because of the ignorance that is in them due to the hardening of their hearts. Having lost all sensitivity, they have given themselves over to sensuality so as to indulge in every kind of impurity, with a continual lust for more.
>
> —Ephesians 4:17–19

Change is to occur as Believers move forward with God and with the help of the Holy Spirit, the grip of the enemy's devices will fall off. Freedom in the Kingdom of God is relevant to the weight of truth applied against strongholds that exist from national and family cultures. Persistent pressure of the words of life and right and just action need to be applied to our life.

THRONE EMPOWERED

In England, where there has been a king or a queen on the throne for centuries, many still do not really understand the power of true kingship, nor do they feel the scope of the power and authority of the meaning of the king's reign. The king and queen in England are not supreme rulers. They are more or less figureheads, loved by the people, and have a minimal amount of authority. In the United States, the president as the commander in chief, is still not a supreme power because he is countered/controlled by the Senate and House of Representatives. Therefore, the free world does not know what is relevant to the reign of kings or kingdoms. Here, we are free to disagree, if we choose. Here people lightly regard their worldly and spiritual freedoms. They have little knowledge of servitude. Here servitude comes with days off, uniforms, at least minimum wages, and usually benefits of some sort.

There are few kings on thrones currently. Many of us, especially in the industrialized world, find it almost inconceivable to know what is involved in the reign of a king—or to understand the kind of power a king wields over a country. So this hinders our grasp of how kingship works and the trustworthiness that belongs to Jesus. Almighty God has supreme power and authority over the natural and the supernatural. Kings rise and fall, but He is Eternal.

In the recent past, the population in a country like Iraq understood that what the ruler said was done, or else! Death to those who oppose a king in different parts of the world is happening even today. To speak out, even in a slight way, will very likely result in that person's head rolling, or hanging from a tree. The king's rules are strictly enforced. Therefore, his reign is complete. People fear the rule of a king in these types of countries. The subjects living there have the mindset to be obedient to what the king says, no matter what. Because they fear the rules of the king and understand his character, these fellow citizens know they will live or die by obedience or disobedience. Friends from these countries bear this out as they have seen public hangings and brother betraying brother. Some countries require Christians to have an identifying stamp on their passport, on their fence, or on their house to let others know that they are different in whom they hold in reverence. In times of war, they put Christians on the front lines before non believers because their worldview is different.

"King" in *Smith's* page 335, means: "A chief ruler, one invested with supreme authority over a nation, tribe or country." In the Hebrew language, king is *malak*, which means to reign, to govern, to rule, to consult, or to counsel. "Kingdom" means "a land ruled by a king." So, the words, "king," "reign," and "kingdom" are archetypes of the same power.

There are kingdoms within the spiritual and natural realm with powers to which each person or social class answers. In both natural and spiritual kingdoms there are kings, princes, principalities, and powers. The supernatural forces that govern in areas have their line of descent. These unseen supernatural forces of good and evil influence people in the natural realm.

In our lives in the natural, the type of kingdom or reign over Believers in reality is not what matters. We are here looking at what is within God's Word that makes freedom possible. It is *relevant* to having Heaven's Kingdom in our life, rather than the country's rule under which we live. Christians in many countries like China have freedom on the inside, but are trapped in a nation that persecutes and kills them. Millions in the United States are in prison emotionally, caught in bondage in their soul, and confined in every way, every day, and handicapped by the media source upon which they've chosen to set their attentions and thoughts. People with burdens (cares small and great) and going through a tribulation in their life without hope, see no way out. People are depressed to the point of committing suicide. They are trapped in emotional and physical bondage. They are locked in these spiritual realms that are only overcome by the amount of God's Truth *each person accepts and obeys.*

Which king will we recognize? Whose reign will we obey? In which kingdom do we want to live? Moreover, will we know how to choose? For whether humankind acknowledges it or not, everyone answers to, that is, bows their knee to someone or something—heads of state, corporate leaders, supervisors, parents, siblings, and on down the line. There is always an order of reign or rule. People everywhere are under some kind of rule that makes up a kingdom. Some territories are bound in culture and tradition so long that it seems impossible to break the iron chains that bind them.

The Bible speaks of several types of kingdoms called "systems" or "ways." There is the kingdom of self, where each one is turned to his own way (see Isa. 53:6). There is the kingdom of this world, where satan is referred to as the prince of this world (see John 14:30). Then there is the Kingdom of the Living God. He owns Heaven and earth and all that is in them (see Isa. 37:16). The entrance to God's Kingdom is Jesus, who is over all kings or kingdoms (see Isa. 9:6–7).

The ways of the human race and satan lead to death. They are referred to as the kingdom of the world. Only Jesus leads to the way of life referred to as the Kingdom of God—or Heaven. Below are a few things listed in the world's kingdom (humankind's and satan's together) and then the Kingdom of the True God (Jesus and God's together). As you read them, add your own discoveries to the two lists that follow, and choose each day who you will follow.

KINGDOM OF THIS WORLD

Limited knowledge and perversions bringing infirmity, death, decay, fear, sadness, mourning, worry (two minds), language with carnal words/ ideas, depression, robbing widows and orphans, stress, overwork, love/ praise of self, lust, control, revenge, hate, coveting, slavery, unbelief, and rebellion.

KINGDOM OF THE TRUE GOD

Unlimited knowledge, supernatural ways of restoring health, life, rejoicing, peace, unity (one mind), good words/ideas, boldness, good mind (cheerful), care of widows and orphans, rest, strength, morality, discipline, forgiveness, freedom, contentment, worship only the God of Truth.

SUPERNATURAL POWER

Freedom to go and preach the gospel of Jesus comes by hearing the good news of Jesus who is a supernatural power, One strong enough to save. Paul tells us, as do the Psalms and Ezra, that Believers do not fight in the natural, but by spiritual powers. Our weapons are not carnal, but are mighty in God for tearing down of strongholds, powers, and principalities (see Eph. 6:12–13), and even overrule death. Confession and praising God are the most germane ways to fight in the spiritual realm.

Enabled by the power of the Holy Spirit, we can choose to stop going in a direction that has separated us from God. Even when Believers learn they are free, it takes a while to stop, turn around, and go in a different direction because the direction we have been going has momentum. It takes a learning process to change direction. We have to stop saying, reading, going, and doing all the things of our old way of life. To change direction is called repenting. Repentance is relevant to the amount of sin that the Holy Spirit reveals to us that we will acknowledge. Repenting means to turn and go another way—God's Way. Our turning to walk fully with God maximizes changes in our character that will reflect the image of Jesus.

For some, drastic changes come quickly once a person chooses Jesus, but more Believers are like me, and we have found change is a process. This new life is a continual journey of experiences that changes our attitudes against the adversary and the way he keeps humanity marginalized in darkness. They know neither the liberty nor the real life that Jesus provided by the cost of His blood. The blood of Jesus is life, for the life of a thing is in the blood (see Lev. 17:11), and it has the ability to speak (see Gen. 4:10; 1 John 5:7–8). Its power actively washes the carnality out of our brain and turns our thoughts and actions to the ways of truth and righteousness. We could say that this is brainwashing, sabotage, and an act of violence in reality. Truth rages against the actions and the knowledge that lead to death, changing the fervor of having the Holy Spirit control our everyday lives. The phrase below gives us a view of our part in the grand scheme of life.

> The world and the people who live on it are in enemy-occupied territory—which is what this world is. Christianity is the story of how the rightful king has landed in disguise, and is calling us all to take part in a great campaign of sabotage.
> —C.S. Lewis, *Mere Christianity,* page 72

When Jesus, the rightful King, came, He gave those who choose Him power to become sons who will rule and who will take back the property that was God's in the beginning. He gives his sons a part as joint-heirs in the victory over the enemy.

BLINDNESS

Because we have learned faith by mixing it with the intellect of the world, corrupt standards keep us weak. Thus, Believers have placed mixed standards over God's Truth. Because there is a spirit of blindness on many Christians in the industrialized world, they only see God in an image of prosperity. However, Jesus said that we will share in his sufferings if we are His (see 1 Pet. 4:12–14). The followers of Christ are beat-up, wounded, and they bleed for their walk with Him. They may experience prosperity, but there is also suffering through which they pass. Only as we live through battles and suffering can we tell others what is applicable in living victoriously.

Currently, many Believers desire a prophetic ministry. They do not realize that such an anointing is trouble rather than fame and fortune.

True Prophets in the Scriptures suffered because they usually brought God's Word to backsliding followers to either correct or encourage. Whatever our gifting, our God is not humdrum. He has exciting things for each Saint to do in this great campaign against the enemy as we join in alliance with Him. We who know God will be strong and do great exploits (see Dan. 11:32). To the extent Believers understand the Lord, He will measure out the mighty acts. God has exploits for us to do in our lifetime. Right now!

DESPERATE FOR ANSWERS

In humankind's desperation for hope, he looks to the ideals of civilization. He proclaims the genius of humans and the power of industry, or he looks longingly to the stars in the solar system. All the while, we boast in living life our way. Many trust in idols, psychic hot lines, or mediums to make decisions for life. Humankind is frantic, running here and there for life's answers. In the instructions in Isaiah 8:19 (paraphrased), the Bible says that when they tell you to consult those squeaking, squawking mediums and fortune-tellers; you are to answer, "Shouldn't a people seek their God? Must the living ask the dead for teaching and instruction?"

This is frightening, as many people, even Christians, rely on the advice of vain gods. They are vain because everything is considered dead if it is not based on the true counsel of the Living God. Saints who do not think as the world does must do one thing—stand unyielding on the certainty of God's Word (see Rev. 2:10; 14:12).

What God says is truth. Truth and untruth are not always common knowledge, and they are not always what we think they are. To understand truth, Saints need to understand what God says about every situation. We must view all things from God's perspective. The three captive Hebrews in the foreign land of Babylon would not bow to the idol of the king. They said their God could save them, and even if He did not, they still would not bow down. We too need confidence in God and not bow to false idols. Believing comes from expecting God to act, just as Shadrach, Meshach, and Abednego did. Even though we cannot intellectually see how to escape peril or how to work out our situation in the natural, we must remain steadfast, trusting in what God can accomplish. We persevere in faith.

Where we set our affections, there too is our heart. Therefore, we should pay attention to what we say when we are away from other

Christians. We can discover whose teachings we bow to, for when we honor someone's instructions, we have gone trembling in their service. For example, if we do what our peers say instead of what Jesus said, we bow in service to them out of fear that we will not please them. The ungodly bow to the world. They are irreverent to the Word of God.

Romans 8:5–8 (paraphrased) says, "For those who are according to the flesh set their minds on the things of the flesh, but those who are according to the Spirit, the things of the Spirit. For the mind set on the flesh is death, but the mind set on the Spirit is life and peace, because the mind set on the flesh is hostile toward God: for it does not subject itself to the law of God, . . . and those who are in the flesh cannot please God."

What we have settled in our mind is relevant—those thoughts that destine us to make public the knowledge of the powers in the world or in God's Kingdom. Saints are living epistles of God's Word. We all are viewed and heard in public like letters read out loud as in days past, when a formal announcement or letter was read publicly in the streets.

When a courier rode right up to the village or town square, the horse's hoofs tossed up puffs of dirt from the road. The guard in the tower alerted the people who dropped whatever they were doing to come and listen. Something different had come into their arena, so they hurried out to hear the tidings. As the rider unfolded the message, the smells of the marketplace beckoned the listeners to come away and sample the wares, but this food was no longer relevant to their needs. The people, eager to see this traveler and hear any news, maneuver among the crowd to get the best view and to bend their ears to hear the message the carrier brings. Sitting straight in the saddle, the herald rings out, loud and clear, for all to understand. This message delivered, the messenger turns his steed and trots off to the next place to proclaim the news.

The messengers of God need to demonstrate and carry good tidings to every place they go. Even when lures of the world call people to turn away—the voice of Believers should be loud and clear. The message is alive and pertinent to bring the hearer understanding and knowledge of the proclamation. Those who listen either accept or reject the news.

Using violent force to take the Kingdom of God is applicable to our understanding, for those who are zealous enough to do things God's way can possess the Kingdom. God's values are not the values of the world. He will increase us if we will give ourselves to increasing His Kingdom. The Scripture says that of those who receive much, much is required, and that those with little who do not use it for God's Kingdom, even that little is taken away and that person is turned over to torturers. The warning has been sounded.

From the written Word of God, we learn of questions each of us needs to ask ourselves, as here in 2 Corinthians 13:5 (NASB). "Test yourselves to see if you are in the faith; examine yourselves! Or do you not recognize this about yourselves, that Jesus Christ is in you—unless indeed you fail the test?" In the CJB, it says it this way, "Examine yourselves to see whether you are living the life of trust. Test yourselves. Don't you realize that Yeshua the Messiah is in you?—unless you fail to pass the test."

To have Jesus found in us is relevant. The valiant ones come up against all odds, but they are valiant because Jesus lives big in them. They understand that what is relevant to God must be relevant to them. They do not yield, but remain faithful, standing strong in the Lord. Their authority comes with status, especially that of a kingship that transcends all others. When the Roman Centurion asked Jesus just to say the word to heal his servant, Jesus was amazed at his trust. The centurion understood what authority demands because he was under authority of a tyrant. He received orders and did them or was thrown in jail or worse. Kingship has this kind of power. Jesus loves the outsider who can understand what God's own people (like many today) do not comprehend. However, the ones who do understand this authority are recognized. They are bold and courageous. They do their part, and God does the part that only He can do.

- How is what is relevant to God pertinent to me?
- If Jesus is my King, how have I served Him?
- Can I see that there are two kingdoms?
- How have my actions changed around the worldly?

Chapter 12

WARFARE: WATCHING
AND WAITING

WHILE READING THE Bible, I noticed there were times when I would sense there was something more—right there that I needed. There was a tug or slowdown pulling in my middle. It was something that just said, *Wait. Don't hurry. I want to show you something.* But because of the fast pace of life or the decision to read a certain amount in a given time, I missed it. I often missed the gold nugget the Holy Spirit had for me. Finally, I learned to stop and pay attention. The Spirit of God is not impressed with my schedule. Obedience is better. He prefers that I stop and look for the nuggets of gold that will help me live the life of the Kingdom that He will reveal. God reveals His secrets to those who are His friends and to them alone (see Psa. 25:14 NLT).

I came across two treasures that are often passed over because they are wrapped up in a story. These are wonderful treasures in plain sight. They are the two weighty subjects of *watching* and *waiting.*

We wait eagerly for the daily news, and once we read or hear it, we stand firmly on its contents. The power of these reports causes many to be fearful of going outside. Anyone out there could be a mad person. They don't wear signs. Compelled, we read or watch the media until we know all the gruesome details of a tragic event. Our minds are crammed with news of the world and every fearful event that happens. People are hungry for news. They gobble it up. While we need to be knowledgeable about events taking place in the world, the news does not have to consume us. We can keep abreast of the worldly news by watching one newscast, reading one newspaper, or reading a little on the Internet.

It isn't just the news. We are also caught up in listening to other things. Even as we ride with others in cars, buses, or trains, we seldom speak to the person next to us. Of course, they may be plugged into a CD player, iPod, computer, or a book. People even go to restaurants and read, and that sends the message they are not interested in conversation. We are caught up in hearing and seeing everything, except God.

After the terrorist attacks on the World Trade Center and the Pentagon, we were all glued to the television. We wondered where terror might strike next. These things are fearful in the natural. At these times, Believers wonder about end-time events. We lack knowledge in the areas of battle in the spiritual realm. Nevertheless, in Jesus we are to know the signs of the times and watch for events at the end of the age, His soon appearing, and those events coming against us in our daily lives. We are watchmen of what God has given us as we stand firm against the attacks of the enemy.

DURING OUR WATCH

What does it mean to have something happen during our watch? This phrase has to do with accountability of events that take place while we are in positions of authority. Even if that authority is just what happens in our own life, our responsibility is to guard what God has given us, as well as those things concerning His appearing.

To know what is happening on our watch, we need to know what God said would come upon the world. What happens on our watch is more than a sign of the end times. It deals with everyday life. Keen-eyed Saints know that waiting and watching are two items of extreme influence with Him, but it is so hard for us to grasp in our fast-paced life. We usually say something like, "I have been waiting for God to move, so why doesn't He answer?" Or on the other hand, "Why don't we see signs and wonders anymore?"

We want it when we want it, which usually means now! Saints who are experienced in faith recognize watching and waiting as warfare. God needs Believers who understand the strategies of fighting a supernatural enemy. From the very beginning, humankind was to watch, guard, and keep possession of the earth, just as Adam and Eve were instructed in the Garden of Eden. God came each evening to commune with them, to give them the correct answer to every question. Instead, they ran ahead of Him. Have you noticed how many times the heroes in the Bible waited? They did not move until they knew God's leading. Watching and waiting produces patience in our life so that Believers do not charge headlong into transgression or fall asleep. Daily, Saints are to look in God's direction, waiting for His instruction in life.

> Blessed is the man who listens to me, watching daily at my doors, waiting at my doorway.
>
> —Proverbs 8:34

WATCHING

There are many areas in our life where watching may surprise us. One of them is found in Luke 12:13–15. "Someone in the crowd said to him, 'Teacher, tell my brother to divide the inheritance with me.' Jesus replied, . . . "Watch out! Be on your guard against all kinds of greed; a man's life does not consist in the abundance of his possessions."

This is a picture of violent watching and guarding that deals with everyday life. Illustrated in the verse above, "watch" denotes the caution needed against anxiety that results from the fear of loss of inheritance. If a Believer frets trying to get things of this world, his thoughts are not on the Kingdom of God. Hope for material possessions or a financial inheritance will separate families. Greed ruling in a person's life can cause harm to everyone it touches. According to the Hebrew meaning (CJB page xxxi), having an *"evil eye," means being stingy*. Greed and stinginess are twins—different names, but the same thought. Be alert against all kinds of evil among which greed is a chief stronghold. Greed traps and snares people in bitterness, hatred, jealousy, envy, and offenses that cause a lack of forgiveness. We need always to be on our guard against such things.

"Watching" is not just viewing an event as a spectator. It takes participation! Watching consists of a place where a person dwells, in the Kingdom of Heaven or the worldly system.

There is also the watching for what is to come in the lives of future generations, as stated here in 1 Peter 1:12, "It was revealed to them that they were not serving themselves but you: when they spoke of the things that have now been told you by those who have preached the gospel to you by the Holy Spirit sent from Heaven. Even angels long to look into these things." In *Young's*, this last sentence reads, "in reference to, which messengers (men or spirits) desire fully to bend alongside of." The one who watches bends forward in eagerness, having a wide view, looking out from a high tower in readiness to see what is happening in the natural and the spiritual realm. Christians spiritually watch from the City of Zion on top of God's mountain. The Kingdom of God envelops our life as we grow and settle in our Promised Land as the pioneers did on the American frontier. Those that watch look out to aid others to observe accurately, judging between bad and good in the world. They are alert and watchful, being sober minded and obeying the commands of the Lord, and they exercise discretion in life. They take time to honor and worship the Lord. They also alert others to what they see.

While a watch is a section of the night, it also involves much more than a period of nighttime watches. The happy of mind (not the worried ones) are those courageous Believers who keep watching. They watch to avoid evil, for evil is always crouching, lurking in the way of life ready to pounce. Evil lies in wait—watching and waiting—to trick the unsuspecting naïve and inexperienced.

There are those who watch for opportunities to share salvation with others, and there are those who are aware of lurking dangers hiding along the way for self and family.

"Watch" in the Hebrew language is, "to be hot! Awake, to rouse self to be alert, watchful. It is a property of one that is alive! A watchman who is not asleep or idle is one who watches and calls out, and the other answers. Psalm 134 tells of those who stand watch through the night in service in God's House." The group that responds knows the answer to the call of those who are watching. Here, both groups are prepared to be the one who watches or the one who answers all have a public voice.

Here the word "watch" also fits the verses that tell Philip to go out to meet the eunuch, and the ten virgins to awake and go out for the Groom is coming. Those who wait and watch are to be ardent and not lukewarm lovers like the Believers at Ephesus (see Rev. 2:4), who lacked their first love. First love is hot! It is alive! Those with the ability to watch, incite others to action. These are the ones who encourage others to buy oil for their lamps. Believers are those who are alert, ready, waiting, and watching for Jesus. They call others to come into the streets to meet the Bridegroom. Violent watching and waiting is a truth we are to learn in the Reign of Heaven.

TIME OF WATCHING AND WAITING

In Hebrew culture, the groom was required to pay a price for the bride. It had to be acceptable to all parties sealing the marriage agreement. Afterward, a covenant marked by a meal confirmed the agreement. The marriage was without consummation between the man and woman. (In the parable of the ten virgins, they represent both men and women because we all receive salvation the same way through repentance and submission to Jesus). Then the groom would give gifts to the bride. Afterward, the groom returned to his father's house to make ready their future home. The groom made provision for his bride's needs while he was gone. Then, when the father knew his son had completed the task at home, he told the son to go get his bride and bring her to the wedding feast. During the waiting time, the bride was to prepare. She was to be always ready, watching, and waiting because she never knew when the groom was returning.

In Hebrew, "watch" also means, "to rub the time away, in the sense of try, proving by rubbing. To search out a matter; to prove it as to test metals. It is used of God in examining the hearts of men." In Job 23:10, "Let Him prove me, I shall go forth like gold," and Job 12:11, "Doth not the ear try words?" These definitions of watch tell of areas of life's battles, and how the interval of time plays heavily in this warfare. Those who know God are strong because of the time spent not only rubbing away in prayer, but also in trials and in the expectation of God's appearing in a situation. The Apostle Paul often said that he stayed in a certain place, not to while away the time on vacation, but he was watching for the leading of the Holy Spirit. In the Greek text in these visits, the words in *Young's* are that he *rubbed the time away*.

WAITING

We see something wondrous in the thinking of God as we wait on Him. As we rely on Jesus to provide, we do not worry about what to say to those over us or about our earthly inheritance or goods that we deserve but have lost. We don't even worry about what we already have. Worry will not add even one hour to one's life. In the Kingdom of God, adding one hour to our life is considered the simplest thing—wow, to add an hour to our life is the simplest thing— then why are we worried about the material things? See how contrary human thinking is to God's thoughts. We must depend on Him. Tomorrow may never come, so it doesn't make sense to worry about what tomorrow *may* bring.

We wait actively and tirelessly, and always knowing that Jesus will come when the time is right. At times, waiting is hard, especially when the days and years go by. We, as the Bride of Jesus, have been looking for His coming for a long time. Absence does not really make the heart grow fonder, as the saying would lead us to believe. Love does not grow unless we are in contact with the one we love. Therefore, we need constant communication with Jesus in an intimate way in order to know and cherish one another.

Waiting on God is a powerful unseen weapon. We cannot give up when waiting for an answer from God. His timing is perfect. To wait on the Lord is a violent act, done in expectant hope and anticipation. Right now, as I write this, I am in a waiting time of preparation for what is to come. If you also are waiting, it may be a time for your preparation. Waiting time is never wasted time. I am beginning to understand that if I am in the place where God wants me to be, it is not necessary that it be a most "wonderful" place. I know I can move, however I am not willing to go until the *Holy Spirit* tells me where and when to go. Going might be all right, but it won't be with the presence of God. What if God comes and I'm not here waiting and watching? Perseverance results in many benefits, one of which is the reward of seeing the foes the Lord will (or has) defeated for me. Another is to witness God's miraculous power to do more than I can imagine as He lets me participate in His work.

God told Moses during the Exodus (see Ex. 33:2–17), to go into the land. He said that He would send an angel with Moses and all would be well. Sounds good, doesn't it? But Moses said, "No I will not go until you go in the lead."

Wow! How bold! Moses expectantly persevered. When God goes with you, nothing is impossible. The result will be more than just good. It will be spectacular! Not too many years ago, I would have said, "God said go and He would send an angel and all will be fine, so here I go." Now I want His presence with me up front. For what will distinguish a person if God's tangible presence is not alongside him? If God's Presence does not go with us, then how are we different from others? When we Believers are uncommon, we are easily recognized. We must be different.

As watchmen, we are to watch and guard against the snares of temptations from the enemy (see Matt. 26:41; Mark 14:38). The hour Jesus will come has not been disclosed. We are to be watching and praying so that we can escape the events that will come upon the world when we are to stand before the Son of Man (see Luke 21:35). We are to stay alert to guard and watch what is going on in all things. He has assigned each of His servants tasks to do, and when He returns, He wants to find every

Believer doing what He asked of them (see Mark 13:33–37) Verse 37 ends with Jesus saying, "What I say to you, I say to everyone: 'Watch!'" This is for all of us—all who carry the name, Christian.

- How can I acquire the gold nuggets of God?
- Waiting is warfare. In my life's battles, how has this weapon been of benefit to me?
- In what events have I eagerly looked in hope for God to send my answer?
- In humbling persevering, what have I done knowing that He is preparing me for great things?

Chapter 13

ASSIMILATED

THE FOREMOST STRONGHOLDS with which every populace of every culture must deal are the unseen forces that lurk around us at all times. These evil forces are weighted chains around our necks—shackles that enslave the mind and war in our flesh as each person is assimilated into the worldview of family, city, and national beliefs.

When I was first confronted with this idea of a *worldview*, I wrestled with the term. I viewed culture as an insufficient hold on people. I thought that by reason and rational thought, people could easily put their culture aside. However, when God started dealing with me, the battle was on. I had no room in my mind for the idea of how forceful culture is. Perhaps you struggle with these concepts too, but once you get the revelation that humankind's view is opposed to God's view, the kingdoms of this world fade and separate from the Kingdom of Heaven.

All my life I truly believed I was following Jesus correctly. However, this revelation of opposing cultures stirred my soul with the breath of new life as I began to think more seriously about two kingdoms: one kingdom of enslaving confusion in the world, the other God's Kingdom of absolute liberty. I thought that it would be possible to retain the good ideas taught in my youth and remain all right in God's Kingdom. I was wrong! With intense study of God's ways, I started to know more of His character and the clear revelation of the light of truth versus the evils of darkness. I realized that my good ideas had to go! Jesus did not think the thoughts of the world when He was on earth. Not at all! Jesus thought and demonstrated the Kingdom of Heaven. Jesus knew the secret of liberty in the natural and the supernatural. He was free to step out of the things that held him and make it possible for those who follow to do the same.

Although He lived in extreme cultures—the Jewish culture, the Roman culture, and the Greek culture—Jesus sought a different way to live—that of dwelling in Heaven on earth. He successfully escaped to a place of liberty, and He changed history for all time! Believers too can escape the surly bonds of these unperceived snares. Let's look at some of the ways of entrapment and of freedom as we investigate several items that we don't recognize as hindrances.

First, we should understand that culture holds us captive by class, gender, language, character, and our attitudes. We are prisoners who fail to recognize our ignorance and blindness to our captivity. From the womb we have never been free of the hold of culture on us. Throughout our life, culture confines us to small spaces.

Before we learn to talk or walk, the current of culture starts its flow into us. Our questions of life arise out of things in our nativity. Our identity arises from the uniqueness of our given name like Tom or Sue, and gives each person distinction. By our surname, we are identified as part of a certain family. And so begins the engineering of our nature. Our characteristics spring from our family, from the people we associate with, and from the culture in which we live, establishing our personality and ideology. Those raised in a certain geographical location share the same ideas or common interests. This is considered one's worldview or mindset.

Today, most people are most interested in their own culture. They often seek to investigate ancestral lineage and the traditions that were practiced in their families of origin. They are eager to have family roots, and they feel the need to resurrect lost heritage if possible. Although God lets us interact and enjoy different cultures, He instructs Christians not to be caught up in genealogy or its pursuit. Even so, it remains of interest within the church.

This training and refining of the moral and intellectual faculties through education form a particular source regarding customs, knowledge, crafts, art, literature, beliefs, and traditions. It locks people into a circle of associates with whom they have limited influence.

Culture captures peoples by national as well as family traditions. People are controlled by what they have learned in their lifetime. Cultural boundaries either shut others out or let them in, making them unacceptable or acceptable. Because of decades of family traditions, resistance to escape is futile. Culture has assimilated humankind into its absolute control.

When we encounter a different culture, our tendency is to deal with it based on our mindset. Why do others think and act the way they do? Can we conform them to think the way we do? We think our way is "one of the ways" or is the "only way," not realizing that for Christians, the only way is the Truth of God.

Our worldview is the way we see ourselves and view the world. We see no need to change unless an admired or feared force persuades us to shift our direction. Throughout the ages of the refinement of people in the world's different cultures, God has been beyond humankind's reach. In fact, we never lift our heads to view God unless God breaks through to us. When a breach happens, it may be so destructive that it terminates the existence of someone or something it contacted. Mightier and weaker vessels cannot exist together without unmerited favor on the part of the one who is mightier. The Almighty God is merciful. He is a consuming fire, and who can live with a continual burning? (See Deut. 4:24; Isa. 33:14; Heb. 12:29). As a consuming fire, He takes no hostages, but with mercy allows us to change our mind and live with Him.

To give a clearer understanding of a breach, lets imagine a boat ride. The water is smooth as glass. The sun is dancing on the surface, and all is serene. On the surface of the ocean, a boat glides through the water leaving V-shaped ripples behind. It seems to be a beautiful placid day. However, unknown to the passengers, there is activity in the ocean beneath them that is about to change their existence. A force lives in the unseen world below. Without warning, the water and air are shattered! Water explodes! Light screams as sound cuts the silence and overpowers the quietness. There right before our eyes is a monster! As a magnificent whale breaks out of its natural realm and into the air, we see an awesome display. How terrifying! Startled by the unexpected leap, the whale's size, and power, we stare with our mouth gaping open. We are motion-less—frozen in time and in wonderment. Except for the rip between the surfaces of two worlds, no destruction occurs when the whale jumps in and out of its domain—that is, unless someone gets in the way. However, if that monster lands on something—it will be devastated. Just as when God breaks in upon humankind, contact with the mighty force of God's visitation gives humankind opportunity to change, to break away from the lifelong boundaries holding us. We sense God's presence and feel His touch, and we are awed that what we could not see becomes real. It may only be that God has glanced in our direction, and just the look of His eyes has made an opening into our realm and brought the experience of the unseen culture of Heaven to earth.

Those that are friends of God, people of renown, have left their old culture and live the life of Jesus Christ (see Phil. 3:9). No longer do they look to what they've known in the past. They are *not* overcome by their ancestry or other worldly cultures. Christians are to have authority and rule over the mores of any refinements of the world. Believers are not here to invite others into the American or any other national ideology. They are, rather, to come out of other cultures that rule over them and live freely here on earth within the culture of the Kingdom of Heaven. God's culture is not like any ancestry on earth, for every culture is in a fallen state and lacks glory. For this reason, God will breach our cultural realm to give us a glimpse of the higher life that is absent.

Christians want to fit God into their lives while remaining unchanged in the journey of life, but God wants our entire mindset to change. If Christians are to live as lights to the world, we must become perfect as our Father is perfect, (see Matt. 5:48). Christians need to turn away from our culture and replace it with God's. We, not God, are the ones going in the wrong direction. We have our thinking thoroughly turned upside-down. This is why we need God's mindset maturing in us as we embrace the mind of Christ.

THE FIRST CULTURE

In Genesis 2:21–23, we read that the LORD God caused the man to fall into a deep sleep. God then took one of the man's ribs, and made a woman from the rib, and man said, "This is now bone of my bones, and flesh of my flesh: she shall be called Woman . . ." (Gen. 2:24). The man was united to his wife, and they became one flesh.

Within God's Garden, Adam and Eve had everything. It was a perfect utopia that included close and intimate friendship with each other and their Creator. The two walked side by side as one unit, as they occupied the Garden. Receiving God's daily counsel, they journeyed together, facing the same direction as did the One True God and just as later Enoch did when he walked with God right into Heaven (see Gen. 5:24; Heb. 11:5), then as, Jesus did when He arose and went to Heaven (see Mark 16:19; Luke 24:51; Acts 1:11; 1 Pet. 3:22), and as later will the faithful (see John 14:3).

Other than in Heaven, the first culture was the one in the Garden of Eden. The name Eden has the Hebrew word *adan* as its root. In Hebrew, *adan*, means "to live delicately, sumptuously, and voluptuously." It means pleasures "to provide a life without hard or rough spots." The garden was to provide its inhabitants a supernatural lifestyle. Adam and Eve's life was supposed to be fulfilled and abundantly happy forever. In fact, within the meaning of flesh is the idea, "to be happy, full, not lacking." It also means to "preach and to proclaim." Therefore, from the very start, a high caliber of lifestyle was set up for humankind's happiness. God's design was for humankind to be pleased; to be vocal and make sounds; to preach and to proclaim to others as a part of their being fruitful and multiplying. Each person was to proclaim God and His instruction on how to live in His Kingdom—under His reign—down through the generations.

Since Adam and Eve counseled with the Creator, the God of all wisdom, they were incredibly intelligent. They had been made in the image of God, and Wisdom had declared that they would have dominion. Every culture of humankind has traditionally placed names on every item—whether inanimate or living. This is an instilled trait designed by God as He brought every beast of the field and every fowl of the air for Adam to name. God wanted Adam to have the privilege of giving names. The name of any thing is not a light matter because the renown of its name is its character. Moreover, once it has a name, it becomes known.

Adam and Eve were to tend, guard, and watch over God's Garden. In their perfect state, their brain capability would have been immense, not the ten percent (less or plus) that humankind now uses. Einstein, considered one of the most intelligent men to live, only used fourteen percent of his brain.

Before Adam and Eve's disobedience, the Garden did not have thorns or briars, the sun didn't burn them, and no rain or snow fell. There was a breeze, but no harsh winds. The Garden was a pleasant thing to care for. Can you see that God's goodness and plans are pleasant toward us?

The Garden contained and sustained every kind of plant and animal life. There were no pesky fungi or anything to cause harm or decay. Work was not considered toil—done by the sweat of the brow—for *hard labor* was unknown at that time. Fatigue is the effect of the fallen state of man. Adam and Eve probably never had joints that ached or sore feet. They worked with great purpose, for they delighted in God. They spoke openly with the King who is above all other kings. Their words carried authority and power. Since Adam and Eve were designed in the image of God, they were covered by the same radiance of God's honor and glory, adorning them with excellence and majesty and with the garments of innocence. Innocent, in the Hebrew language means, "to have a protective covering from soil." It means, "to be counted pure, to be translucent, clothed, but naked. To be free and with benchmark beauty." Adam and Eve were innocent and without a hard or dark spot in their hearts. They had favor with the Highest authority.

Humankind's disobedience to God and sin against humankind made them miss the goal of eternal life. Death immediately ensued, taking humankind by force on the way toward death. In dying daily they eventually died utterly. Adam and Eve lost their shared authority with God. It was the unimaginable cost of defiled purity. They darkened their unsheathed innocence with smudges of sin as their glory began to fade. Power in every aspect of humankind's life became weakened. Adam and Eve lost interest in the intimate relationship with God that is necessary to have truth and freedom. It was another sign of their fallen nature. The distance between each generation and God increased to the point that when their grandsons were born, there was the need to invoke the Lord (see Gen. 4:26), for if they desired the counsel of a Friend, they needed to *call out* for God to come.

God's daily dwelling was no longer with them for friendship and counsel. Their eyes were now cast down to view only the world of fallen natures instead of the views of Heaven.

A THING THOROUGHLY SET DOWN

In Genesis 2 God had already given instruction for when a man and woman marry. It is a matter thoroughly set down (command) as to the correct perspective regarding marriage. Man marries a woman. Female and male come to live together and multiply, bearing a family and being fruitful in developing the traits of godliness. The *man* is to leave his father and mother and cling tightly to his wife as they become one. He leaves what he knows from his growing up years. He works toward becoming one-minded with his wife. Even prior to Adam and Eve having children, they received the command to pass this instruction on to the people who would follow. The command is that each person is to leave the way of their parents who dwell in the kingdom of the world, forsake all others, and consult with the Father in Heaven—just as Adam and Eve had done at first.

Man and woman united to become one in their ideas of the views of God. We, the Bride of Jesus, are to bind ourselves to Him as our only Beloved. We are not to chase after strange lovers. As it is in Heaven, so it should be here on earth. It says in Song of Solomon, "My Beloved is mine and I am my Beloved's." The binding should be so tight that nothing can distract us from our necessary relationship with Jesus.

After all, The Creator made Eve to be a help "meet." In the Hebrew, "meet" means "good, beautiful." Working to fit Adam, she was comparable to him, or suitable as drawing praise—due reward. And in *Young's* it says, "as his counterpart, literally, 'One over against him' corresponding to him." She was not less than Adam. They were united, both just as worthy as the other one. Humankind separates male and female; but God is no respecter of persons.

Husbands are to support their wives in making decisions that are *in order with the Word of God*. Adam was commanded not to eat of the tree of good and evil. He would be the one to relate the command to Eve. He listened, but did not hold tight to his wife and support her against the question/interrogation that the adversary raised against God's Word (see Gen. 3:17). Adam gave consent to what the serpent said by his *silence*. The Old Testament supports this, as God says that when the man allows what is not God's perspective and the woman does it, then the man is at fault.

Leaving Flesh Behind

Moses and Zipporah both had to change their lifestyle and mindset and turn to God's way. As they started out following *I AM that I AM*, a circumcision had to take place. Unneeded flesh, the flesh of a carnal mindset had to be eliminated. One meaning of covenant is to cut; a cutting had to be made with God. This act of circumcision was imperative for all followers. It is now a circumcision of the heart (see Rom. 2:28–29). Being born in a Hebrew home, Moses had been circumcised on the eighth day. Now the circumcision of his and Zipporah's son was necessary. The act of this circumcision affected Moses and Zipporah's fleshly understanding in their dealings with God (see Ex. 4:25–26). Cutting off all ancestral roots, they would have to leave behind everything they knew to go into uncharted territory. This is the charge and challenge of mission Exodus! Actually, this act of cutting off ancestral roots separated them in life. There is no evidence that either she or the children went through the wandering in the desert nor is there any indication they died in the desert. Moses continued to live the life of an army officer, fighting battles, and Zipporah returned home to raise their family. They probably never saw each other again on earth. Many times, when a missionary goes to the front lines of battle, someone stays behind to raise the family. Family members may only meet again in Heaven.

Whether the man and woman both go to the front lines in full-time service or not, the act of letting go of the hold of the world is an act each has to appropriate. There are Christians who may be tortured or martyred for bringing the good news. Forging into the violence found in the hearts and minds of lost humanity is an act of unselfish love. To change humankind's direction of assimilation for eternity, these Believers will brave all obstacles to liberate humankind with the only news that is powerful enough to restore life. Going into hostile territories where people hate them, missionaries enabled by the force of the Holy Spirit break strongholds that hold humankind hostage. They pull down vain imaginations in the hearts of a dark mindset. They lead captivity captive (see Rev. 13:10).

- How can I distinguish the world's cultures from the culture of Heaven?
- What does it take to become one-minded with Jesus?
- The culture of Heaven is not like any other. How can I take captivity captive with its truth and freedom?

Chapter 14

STRANGE LIPS VS. RELEASE IN CITIZENSHIP

RELEASE BEGINS WITH words that come from the Word of God. Jesus Christ, our role model, is the living example for a successful life here on earth. He struggled against the same forces that all humans do—the supernatural forces around each person and the secrets hidden in the deep recesses of the mind/heart. Even His own family thought He was out of His mind (see Mark 3:21). Jesus did things no one else had done. He spoke as no one ever had. His language was out of this world. His citizenship was in Heaven. As Saints, our habitation is also not of this world. Therefore, our response to events and words should be different. They should not display our carnal nature but the nature of Jesus.

There is a battle, and it rages mostly in our thoughts—thoughts that are filled with unbelief and words that negate what we have heard about truth. Our words often battle the confidence in our heart. This fight against unbelief seems impossible to win in the natural mind, but with courage and aid from the Holy Spirit, our mission is possible. Because of vain imaginations, even Saints have to struggle with wrong thoughts. However, we do not have to let these thoughts overpower us. Struggling against wrong thoughts is not a task in futility. It is just the old nature trying to keep us in captivity. Since we get our directions from Heaven, our mission in this land/earth will be victorious. Living here, we are not in bondage to the lies of the evil one. Before we occupy this land, we must learn the language of the Kingdom. We must pass through tests and trials and prove that we understand the words of God in our heart. Our reactions to tribulation in life control how we handle our present. When deliverance comes, the experience establishes power to be unyielding in a present situation and a foundation for trials to come. Trials will come;

life is all about surviving what happens. Like the saying goes, "What doesn't kill us makes us stronger." As new creations, we have been given the freedom and abundant liberty Jesus has secured for us. Freed from sin's power over us, our mind, having been established with the mind of the Liberator, nothing is impossible for Saints united with Jesus Christ.

After Jesus is commissioned, the adversary subjects Him to enormous test. Here is one of these tests in Luke 4:5 (CJB):

> The Adversary took him up, showed him in an instant all the kingdoms
> of the world . . .

No human knows the total vastness of each test Jesus endured. Those tests were beyond human comprehension. Saints come face to face with what will try us to our full measure. However, God has promised He will not allow His beloved to be tempted beyond what each can bear (see 1 Cor. 10:13).

With Jesus' response to each of the tests mentioned in Luke there is release from the enemy's power to tempt Jesus in that area. The beginning of release for Jesus public ministry started with His biggest temptations. Our release will come the same way. Words bring release. This testing was a violent act, and Jesus met His tempter with an even more violent act. He used words of certainty. Jesus met half-truths with the power of complete truth! Even though the enemy used Scripture, Jesus knew the full story. Although the adversary had seized the kingdoms of the world, Jesus knew the enemy is the father of lies (see John 8:44).

Jesus remained one in essence and substance with God the Father of Truth (see John 8:18). Unyielding, He resisted the deceiver. By wielding words sharper than a two-edged sword, Jesus cut down the violent persuasions of His tempter. Speaking words of destruction upon the fallacies satan presented, Jesus not only spoke the same thing with God, but He acted on them by not falling down to worship the devil. In obedience, Jesus spoke words—powerful words that live as a testimony for Christians down through the ages. Christians will be tried and tested as was Jesus. We overcome the enemy by confessing words that are certain and completely sound. The courageous know which land they dwell in, and they speak its language.

The minds of non-believers rest on quicksand, and their thoughts are stuck in a land of murkiness stained with greed, lust, and self. Released from this prison of powerless, godless jargon, we are not in its captivity any longer. Light bursts the darkness of ignorance that comes from earthly views. Speaking truth frees us from lies and the chains of guilt and shame.

The natural man cannot speak from the viewpoint or mindset of the spiritual man unless he has knowledge of the spiritual. Carnal people do not hear what the True God says, for they are listening to their father, the god of this worldly system.

> They are from the world; therefore, they speak from the world's viewpoint; and the world listens to them. We are from God. Whoever knows God listens to us; whoever is not from God doesn't listen to us.
> —1 John 4:5–6 (CJB)

Believers have the choice to believe humankind or God. Worldly views and languages are innate and please the flesh and the soul (mind). Worldly people act or react to a situation and usually have no desire to change. It is one thing for Christians to listen to and understand what the world says while realizing that it is not what God says or desires for humankind; it is another matter when Christians are in agreement with what the world says and does. When people are not interested in the language and concepts of God's Kingdom, they choose instead to listen to familiar words of the world, and they fail to live the standards of Heaven. They are not Christians, but dry clouds (see 2 Pet. 2:17–19). The language of our Promised Land and the knowledge and willingness to stand firm on what the Word says is important. It is how Saints distinguish the Spirit of Truth from the spirit of error. Deceptive words come from the world's viewpoint. Release comes when we speak the words of truth. These words of truth overcome the false words we have heard and spoken. Eventually truth changes the deeds we do.

Where we get our news and information helps form our words and ideas. In the natural, the noises of the world look and sound good. These words and ideas carry the authority we give them. Language comes out of the world, self, or from God, and it showers down into our ears. In the same way a steady dripping of water will eventually bore a hole or make ripples in a rock, a steady stream of words will eventually engrave their signature in us and will bring from our heart what the mouth speaks. Words form a person's attitudes and behavior.

This may seem a little overwhelming. It may seem impossible with man, but with God, *all things are possible* (see Matt. 19:26; Luke 18:27, emphasis mine). We have help. We are not alone. We have the Comforter alongside us, so stop and start again. In the same way we learn to drive a car, sometimes it takes many stops and starts on the journey of life to get it right. We do not learn all we need to know in one attempt. It took time in preparation, practice, and dedication.

I grew up with siblings who could give in words as good as they got. It wasn't always vicious, but it was smart-mouthed. Words were common such as, "Hey, I'm smart," the response was, "Yeah, smart aleck." However, from God's point of view, this sort of language is to take each other lightly, to tread on or to look down on someone. This habit of a quick retort became so natural that the overflow came out of our mouth before we thought about it. It was we siblings' cultural mindset. This seemed pretty harmless and funny, but it did not produce good fruit in walking with God. For me, it took constant reproof, refining, and the training of my thoughts to put the brakes on this type of communication.

In a further illustration of how language turned upside-down traps us in our worldly tradition, the following is an actual conversation of several Christian people sitting around in a break room:

> First woman speaks; rubbing her hands together: "My hands ache!"
>
> First man asks: "Do you have arthritis?"
>
> First woman with acceptance in her voice: "Well, my mother and grandmother both have it, so I'll inherit it."
>
> Second woman interjects: "No, don't you know you've been redeemed from inherited curses? You have a new inheritance in Christ Jesus."
>
> First woman retorts, almost in defense of disease and indignant greed to have her family inheritance besmirched: "My family has arthritis and I get everything they have!"
>
> Trying to encourage, the undaunted second woman, replies, "You know that by your mouth you bless or curse."
>
> There is silence.

There could have been a different scenario. The first woman could have said something that a Saint would say, something *not of this world.* Reminding herself of what the Lord has done in building up her trust in Jesus' healing ability. "My hands ache, but Jesus has provided healing. Jesus healed so and so of cancer, so I know God heals. Thank you, Jesus, for healing me." On the other hand, she might have asked the other Christians to pray for her. This is a very important step for healing and to begin the release from these unseen forces of language that hold our nativity to this world.

It is strange that people, even Christians, almost revel in holding onto something, even sickness, when we can connect it to family or society. We pay no attention to what Jesus provides and we forget that we belong to His family. Now, no one likes aches and pains, but we do not want to give up our inherited infirmities. Even if they are killing us by the language used, we continue to claim what plagues us as our own. We do not want to give up what we feel in the natural. It is easier to believe what our flesh is saying. We also accept what our family says without doubt. By remaining steadfast in what we feel and see, we deny what is ours in the spiritual that will affect the natural.

Even if we remain steadfast and immediate relief does not happen, we must continue to confess, rightly trusting the Word of God. For it is by hearing the Word of God that faith comes and by believing that God's reward is on the way. What we have ears to hear with comprehension strengthens us. Sometimes it takes years to confess and not deny healing. By experience healing comes! It is by speaking in faith that we please God, and it is He who brings deliverance.

Yes, blessing and cursing is in our mouth. As we speak good out of our mouth, we pour out blessing on the heads of humankind. Blessing has in its meaning *to speak well and good*. To curse is *to pour out evil and bad*. Changing our words will help us slow down the direction in which we are going, and will turn us in a forward direction with God. Then, as we confess and believe, "I have a *new* inheritance of healing, thank you," we initiate a foundation of trust in God's Truth.

Jesus became a curse so that Saints can be set free from any family inheritance. All natural inheritance of family is fallen and in a cursed state. Jesus has brought us back to wholeness. By His stripes and by His blood we have healing and life—complete life, not the weakened life affected by sin.

Words coming from a carnal man have no guarantee, and every word of the devil is a lie! Failing to acknowledge God's Truth and wisdom is different than what we have already attained growing up. Because the Word of God is under full warranty, it is totally reliable! With its mixed standards, carnal thinking is completely opposite. So with carnal ideas we continue toward confusion and destruction. As we start to believe, we struggle to make room in our mind for this new extreme truth. Wrestling with God, we change. We are unable to walk in the world as we once did.

God's people suffer violence by being ignorant of God's ways. As part of His Kingdom, we are to operate the same way on earth as life operates in Heaven. By our refusal to read the manual that God has given us, we do not know our potential! We lack our Father's eyes to see from Heaven's prospective, and we continue to inherit humankind's fallen state. Without fully understanding what freedom is, we underestimate our new inheritance. Jesus has redeemed us completely!

When Saints continue to speak the words of the world, we reestablish belief in them. We trust what we hear. The world will reign in us instead of the Kingdom of Truth. Correcting our mouth initiates new thinking in us, which leads to new actions. Our mouth speaks from words established in our heart. His words must be active in our heart, not just in our head and mouth. It is not easy, but Jesus has given us the power to overcome. Therefore, when we start to rebuke our old words by laying the weight of sound words upon them immediately, the old words resist. They also prepare to leave. Continued rejection of the old words forces them completely out of our minds. This violent act starts to pull down those high places in the mind with the weight of truth. So, action is working with faith as we wait expectantly for changes in our lives.

We find that help is not distant, but right here in our mouth! As in Romans 10:8, 10 (CJB), "The word is near you, in your mouth and in your heart,"—that is, the word about trust which we proclaim, . . . For with the heart one goes on trusting and thus continues toward righteousness, while with the mouth one keeps on making public acknowledgement and thus continues toward deliverance.

Notice how these verses say, *continues toward* righteousness and deliverance. As Believers go forward into the reality of the Kingdom of Heaven, we leave behind the ways of the kingdom of this world. We progress by continued action and confession and by watering the seed of faith God has given each one of us. Thinking like God results in working yoked together with Christ (see Matt. 11:29–30), but it will be light work. The language of the world involves unjust strongholds that we have to battle and tear down. New strongholds, towers of righteousness, are established in us for the reign of the Kingdom of God. Do not become discouraged if this is a slow process. Our new mindset is being conformed to the image of Jesus (see Rom. 8:29).

Not knowing or being in doubt is to be of two minds. It is a "que sera" attitude, neither cold nor hot. Saints are to have one mind that is united with Christ Jesus. Our desire is to be set on His Kingdom and working under His authority. The spiritual realm will know that we know what authority backs our confession. In fact, the supernatural realm will know before we know, as we see when the demons in Acts 19:15 (NASB) said, "I recognize Jesus, and I know about Paul, but who are you?" The demons knew who backed Jesus and Paul, and they had to obey and leave. Jesus was acquainted with evil and evil knew Him. Every evil knew that Jesus had authority over them. Will the demons recognize us?

Personally, I never realized the grip that old habits had on my words and life until I tried to quit some of them—things like carnal ideas, music, words, and etc. Why don't you try it? Why don't you try to pull away from worldly views and language, and you too will see the hold they have on you. You will be amazed at how difficult it is to break free, just as I did.

God puts great value on words. For with words He creates. In fact, if the Creator speaks anything, it happens. God has also identified Jesus as the Word (see John 1:1).

Agreement on the meaning of words, as well as how words will be used, is necessary for all the parties involved to understand and be guided into unity (see Rom. 15:5). Jesus commanded Saints to be united in the same way He and the Father are united (see John 17:21–22). Without agreement, communication becomes confusing and difficult, if not impossible.

As one of his first goals, Alexander the Great had to unite the Greek tribes to build an empire. When Alexander traveled from one township to another in the Greek nation, he soon discovered that each community had its own tongue. They had molded their own distinct communication. Different dialects were at the heart of the nation's disunity. Alexander masterfully commanded all tribes to learn a common Greek language. With unity under one language, he conquered and possessed the known world.

Because the language spoken and understood by people determines their citizenship, Saints entrenched in the language of God solidify their citizenship in Heaven where no worldly thoughts or deeds exist. While living here on earth, we start to understand that this unseen force of united words establishes us in the Kingdom of Heaven because it changes those who use it as they gain revelation of heavenly views. Our priestly anointing increases as our citizenship is established, resulting in the Father's business done on earth as it is in Heaven. While unity in understanding worldly knowledge enables confusion to be entrenched deeper and deeper, this estrangement keeps Saints from doing as Jesus said and did.

GOD'S WAYS WORK ANYWHERE

The Islamic belief requires everyone to learn the Koran in the original language. This unites them in words and belief. Muslims have grasped this concept for establishing their citizenship in the reign of Islam.

The Living God's concepts work, no matter who uses them. God rains on the good and the bad. His sun rises on all humankind. Any passionate person has the opportunity to take the Kingdom by force.

When the Hebrew slaves returned from Babylon to rebuild the Temple in Jerusalem, Ezra ordered that the Hebrew men leave their foreign wives and children. The wives, who taught their children, had learned the Hebrew language, but their understanding was Babylonian. The effect was to have strange lips, because even though they could speak the Hebrew dialect, their thoughts were impure, and they understood Hebrew with perverseness. Just as today when Christians mouth the words of Scripture, they understand it in the language of the culture of the world. To say in our words today "that's bad" means its good, whereas the real meaning of the word *bad* means below standard, poor, or unfavorable. On the other hand, saying something like "subway" could be a sandwich place or in New York the electric train below the streets. Of course, in London, they call the train "the tube," and a subway a walkway under a street. To understand the words of the Bible correctly, a study of Hebrew, Chaldee, and Greek will help, as God chose these languages to set down in writing what He wanted to relate to His people. The Helper, the Spirit of Truth, brings to life the Scripture and guides us as we study. He empowers us to know and effectively understand the words of Heaven. Now free, our mouth defines our citizenship, as our conversation relates the ways of Heaven (see Phil. 3:20).

The beginning of release comes when Christians recognize that sin is weaker than we are. He that lives in us is stronger than he that is in the world (see 1 John 4:4). Those who travel the narrow way, speak and act like Heaven. They believe the Truth of God over the truth of the world. The bold and courageous do not sound like others. They do not act like others. They are out of their minds, for they have the mind of Christ.

Modern day missionaries Heidi and Rolland Baker heard about a country where the population was being terrorized and where every evil thing imaginable was occurring, including multiple killings. The people fled for their lives. The wife said to her husband, "Let's go there," so they did. They laid down their lives to show the love of Jesus in this world. Their citizenship is in Heaven, so they speak and do as Jesus would.

- Where does my language put my citizenship?
- How can I improve my necessary relationship with God?
- When should I ask for prayer?
- Without sounding religious, how can I speak God's Truth?

Chapter 15

SHREWD: NOT A BAD WORD

WHEN THE WORD *shrewd* is used, it often brings to mind someone cunning or underhanded—attributes that deal with the violence done to humankind. It portrays a person who is cruel, hurtful, brutal, and mean-natured. This kind of person, being as venomous as a snake, would take what he wanted. One who is shrewd has a hidden malicious agenda. He is void of integrity. A person who may appear to help others might really want something for their own gain. Such actions might be considered good business in a world that appreciates the astute person who knows how to get ahead. However, God is not pleased with any person who is shrewdly violent in this manner.

Our thinking adapts easier to good business in God's Kingdom if we know that shrewd also means the same as *prudent*. In *Webster's,* prudent means, "To be wise in practical affairs; careful, cautious in the regard to danger; springing from practical wisdom. It means to be judicious which means to be characterized by sound judgment." This definition lends itself very easily to discernment in everyday life.

We see it in Proverbs 1:4–5, "For giving prudence to the simple, knowledge and discretion to the young—let the wise listen and add to their learning, and let the discerning get guidance."

When Christians look at the prudence of God, we have a hard time thinking that it works, because our training is in the reasoning of the world's standards. The people in the kingdom of the world have influenced us all our lives. Believers are immersed in the ways of the world and are molded by its ideas. Most of the beloved have learned to get ahead by pursuing life the world's way. Using rules that reign in the standards of earth, we have tried to adapt God's ways to what we already know. This is wrong. We cannot mix values! We must be relentless to put old ways to death, and then to put godly instructions in their place as we walk in new life and faith.

Jesus never used the world's way of thinking. In fact, Jesus sent Peter to get money, not from the bank—well, the bank of the river or lake—for gold. Gold out of the mouth of a fish! This is common sense in the Kingdom of Heaven. After all Heaven's streets are paved with gold. The cleverness of God is that we should laugh at enemies and speak to trees to produce fruit. We should put mud on blind eyes to see. It is impossible by our traditions or intellect to do this kind of ministry. It has to be done as Jesus did it—through close relationship to Abba Father (literally, His Daddy). Jesus used the harmony of His Father's thoughts, words, and actions to represent His image.

The missionary George Mueller often had no food for all the orphans in his care. He would have the table set, have them all sitting down at the table. After a prayer of thanksgiving had been said, food would arrive at the door. His common sense, which meant having an understanding heart of Heaven's values, set his belief in God to supply all their needs.

If we begin to do what Jesus did, life gets very interesting. If we are bored, this will change things, because trying to do what Jesus did will change everything in our life. As we stop seeing the enormity of the world and start seeing what Heaven sees, we experience the power of God moving in our life and work.

The shrewd or prudent person will be teachable. They will be willing to learn. In fact, they will search every word or act to see if it is of God. We cannot expect the Word of God to just come into our mind. One time I was given the books of Isaiah and Ezekiel in a dream. I believed that the contents of those books would miraculously be in my mind in the future. I was wrong. When I came to my senses and decided to start reading Isaiah, I soon found Isaiah 34:16 (NASB) where it says, "Seek from the book of the LORD and read." This verse came alive to me. This was the proof I needed. My part was to research the Book of the Lord, and in His timing, understanding would be given. We are all simple and foolish when it comes to knowing the ways of the Kingdom of Heaven. Common sense of the wisdom of God tells us in Proverbs 8:5, "You who are simple, gain prudence; you who are foolish, gain understanding." So listen to what the Word says, because it's learnable! Luke 16:8 (NASB) says that the sons of this age are more shrewd in relation to their own kind, than the sons of light.

People of the world are the sons of this age. They are shrewd (more astute) in how to get the best, while Saints who are the *sons of light* do not know. Because we try to succeed the way the world does by doing the same things, we are to know how the rules of Heaven work instead of only practical things of the world. It seems that common sense is rare today. Even the understanding of nature has been redefined and commercialized. Humankind's whole aim is to be comfortable and have more than we need. It is sad, but true, that the Sons of God do not know the rules of the Kingdom of God. Christians are waiting to receive in Heaven or waiting for their needs to miraculously appear while suffering and wonder why God does not deliver. Continued ignorance of the Scriptures keeps Saints powerlessly living life the way the world does. Our Heavenly Father wants us to receive a happy and pleasant life, and to be content in whatever condition we find ourselves (Phil. 4:11, Heb. 13:5).

The complete verse below in the CJB is a little more extensive than the above NASB verse and may be easier to understand.

> And the employer of this dishonest manager applauded him for acting so shrewdly! For the worldly have more "*sekhel*" [intelligence, common sense] than those who have received the light—in dealing with their own kind of people!"

God's Children, the Sons of Light, cannot treat others the same way as those in the world do. As in the verse above, those of the world still applaud dishonesty, crime, and distrust. People have not changed since the introduction of sin into the world. Humankind remains the same. Because of what we see and feel in the world, a clear view of Heaven is hard to keep in mind. Throughout history, the Hebrews wanted to do as the children of the world did, and just as Christians do today! But children of light are supposed to find out what and how Heaven treats others. They are to do that which Jesus did while He was here on earth. Jesus is the door through which Saints view the workings of Heaven on earth.

The world, out of a need to achieve, considers first the outcome for self and material gain. Our Counselor used the wisest man in the world, King Solomon, to leave practical guidelines for any who will read and apply them. The meaning in *Young's* for *proverbs* is "ruling things, superior things, and matters for living our life." As we look at any part of the Book of Proverbs, we find practical applications for our daily life. The proverbs lay out Heaven's manifested rule from God for our lives. Below are two examples:

> When the righteous prosper, the city rejoices; when the wicked perish, there are shouts of joy.
>
> —Proverbs 11:10

> Misfortune pursues the sinner, but prosperity is the reward of the righteous.
>
> —Proverbs 13:21

The shrewdness of God is very practical. God is not out there in a mystical fuzzy-wuzzy way. The Living God is in the now. He is timeless and always present. He is interested in the practical matters of life, such as our health and in making provision for us. God desires that we too have an enjoyable and abundant life, one that is heart-centered. His way of achieving this is not the way we have learned from a world wrapped up in self-life.

As we look into these rulings words, God will give us direction for every area of life.

RIGHT THINKING

Look at this story in the Luke 17:7–10 which concerns a slave who has labored all day. Jesus uses a parallel of the worldly employer who wants the employee, after working all day, to change his clothes, bathe, and feed him (the employer). However, this should not be. As the story continues, it shows Heaven's view, in which employers are called to go the extra mile for their employees and treat them as they would like to be treated. How radical! How upside down—or should we say, right side up. In the world, employers never think of switching places with an employee or servant. After all, employers are over employees and they want the employees to understand that they are subservient. But that is not God's view or thoughts. Heaven's view sees the leader as the one who serves those whom he oversees (see Matt. 20:28; Mark 10:45; 1 Pet. 5:2), making sure they have what they need for a pleasant life while in their service to him.

Jesus said that if you want to be the leader, you must be the servant of all (see Mark 9:35). A picture of leadership is seen in the story of Stephen, when he was selected to serve tables—not because he is incapable of establishing churches, but because he is a leader! Stephen is such a leader that when he preaches, they stone him to death. Bearing the nature of Jesus, Stephen asks God to forgive those who are killing him. That's a leader! What kind of leadership did that show those who were standing there, such as the one holding the coats, the Pharisee, Saul of Tarsus? There is a sharing in both the glory and the suffering of Christ. This balance of suffering and honor brings great weight to bear against the lightweight character of the carnal. Bringing evidence of what is to come, the Spirit tells Saul of Tarsus how much he must suffer (see Acts 9:16) for God's namesake. I'm sure Saul remembered the suffering of Stephen and looked to the boasting of God's glory (Rom. 5:2–3). As Paul lived and suffered for the name of Jesus, Paul remained humble, giving all glory to God. This is an act of violence to our thinking.

God's Kingdom is opposite of the kingdom of the world. In some instances, the truth is so extremely opposite, that I, for one, have had to get radical with all my words, actions, and thinking. Jesus showed the disciples how to lead as He washed their feet. A leader serves others. Jesus powerfully demonstrated what He wanted to be lived out here on earth. He led by example and by demonstrating with spoken words. He used radical faith to be what no one else could be. Everything had to go, even for this Son of Man, because Jesus had left all His glory when He came to earth (see Phil. 2:6–11). He came for glory—for God's praise—because all have fallen short of the glory of God (see Rom. 3:23). To show God's glory, Jesus demonstrated how a person looks, acts, talks, and walks. Christians are called to be ruthless in vanquishing the fallen nature, so the missing glory and honor can be ours. Quite often, it takes some doing to get all of our old nature out of our life. Taking authority over our old nature often comes slowly. Our strength grows as the ravages of our old nature are defeated. Even though we have the Kingdom of God in us, the kingdom of the world still has possession of a large portion of property within us. It will take constant persistence through the Holy Spirit to remove the kingdom of the world from our lives. God is not going to take from any of us what we are not willing to give. This is not self-determination. This is letting go and dying to our self-life. It is asking, repenting, forgiving, and asking for more of the Holy Spirit to take control and overflow our life.

COMMON SENSE

. . . for acquiring a disciplined and prudent life, doing what is right
and just and fair.

—Proverbs 1:3

This proverb tells us why we should attain wisdom and knowledge—
for deeds of justice and righteousness. To reject this wisdom and discipline
is to be a fool/easily swayed. God is prudent and practical about laying out
all the good and evil ways before us, so that we will discern the difference
and possess the promises of God.

Psalm 18 says that the wicked will be defeated because God is shrewd.
To confound or confuse the wise in the world, God defeats enemies by
confusion. He routs them. He treads on them, and God slays them by
the blasts of His nostrils. These are only a few of His tactics. Then God,
our Provider, gives Believers the spoil! What would He do with the
spoils of humankind? To be shrewd, God's way is totally upside down
in our universe. The clever precepts of the Mighty One are beyond our
thinking. Just look at how He artfully schedules the events of the Exodus
of the Hebrews.

But I will harden Pharaoh's heart, and though I multiply my miraculous
signs and wonders in Egypt.

—Exodus 7:3

This is common sense right-side up. Who in this world would want
to succeed by making a higher authority mad? If we think it would be
easy, try it on our employer or family. Moses asked that Pharaoh let the
Hebrew slaves go to worship their God for three days. This angered
Pharaoh. However, in wisdom, Adonai leaves nothing to chance. Nor
does He leave anything incomplete. Neither will He put his plan into
inexperienced hands because He desires a certain end.

Again He says in Exodus 14:4, "'And I will harden Pharaoh's heart,
and he will pursue them. But I will gain glory for myself through Pharaoh
and all his army, and the Egyptians will know that I am the LORD.' So the
Israelites did this."

The wondrous God tells Believers only what we can handle and what
gets our attention, letting nothing confuse us: such as details on how
He will work it out. Can we imagine that the sea would part and the
entire army would rush in and drown? Of course, the fact that the army

would chase the fleeing Hebrews into the sea was left out of the blueprint given Moses. Why scare him? The ways of God are usually beyond our comprehension and probably stop our obedience. God will bring about the miraculous if His people will just do the portion He tells us to do.

He then says in Exodus 14:17–18, "I will harden the hearts of the Egyptians so that they will go in after them. And I will gain glory through Pharaoh and all his army, through his chariots and his horsemen. The Egyptians will know that I am the Lord when I gain glory through Pharaoh, his chariots and his horsemen."

However, when caught up in the events, people don't view them the same way. To the Israelites it looked as if they would be defeated. They thought their destruction was inevitable. After the fact, we can see the full measure of God's shrewdness as He uses everything that is against Him for the renown of His name. The result brings glory and honor to God alone in a way that surpasses the imagination of humankind. Wouldn't God at least keep the chariots and horses for the Believers to use? God thought differently, wanting it all devoted to Himself. Everything was destroyed. He made the defeat of the enemy so complete that the nations knew the fame of the One True God. They had heard of this terrible fearsome God! It was not the Hebrews they feared, but that *they have a fearsome God.* After all, God does not fight fair. He always wins and takes no captives!

Another example is in the life of Jacob, where at an appointed place, for once in Jacob's life, God had his full attention. This powerful experience changed Jacob's life and gave the glory to God.

Some say that Jacob fought with God and won. However, examine the Scripture and see that Jacob, tired of his messed-up life, asks for a new identity. He knew he could not continue on the old road he was traveling. What was the actual prize that Jacob won? The Writings, commonly known as the Bible, tells us that the thing Jacob won was that Adonai was now *his* God and not just his father's God. The Lord God would be with him as He had been with his father. Jacob leaves the fight a broken and contrite man before God. He has turned from his violent scheming ways to go in a new direction. Jacob is crippled physically, and he is in fear that he will not be able to talk his twin brother Esau out of killing him. Jacob is an amateur to these new ways of the Kingdom of Heaven and remembers the traits of their family, so he goes in a different direction. Or Esau may have attempted to pull Jacob back into their old lifestyle. Jacob must have realized that bad company corrupts good intentions. God showed His shrewdness at this point in Jacob's life. Now, the God of

Isaac is the God of Israel. The new identity that Jacob won changes his life and forces him to walk a different path than his brother.

Heroes know their God and look for His action in the events of life. They keep a keen eye open for the unusual things God will do on behalf of those who are known by Him. They expectantly wait the birthing that will come as an effort of waiting and doing exactly what the Holy Spirit instructs. They keep their spiritual eyes on Jesus. Not all things seem sensible to the valiant of God, but they act upon whatever the Spirit says. They thank Him in all things. People destroy their homes, beat them up, and leave them for dead just for giving out tracts of the good news. Later on, however, they meet people who came to Jesus because of what they witnessed these Saints going through for love.

One such man is Henry Gruver, who vowed he would hand out a certain number of tracks each day. He was spit upon, threatened, and cursed. Because of obedience to God's counsels, and His faithful acts, God placed Gruver in front of royalty—even in their palaces. As he prayer walks in foreign lands, he is trusted with more of the Kingdom. Heroes gain glory and honor given only by God, not humankind. It is God who lifts up a person before kings.

- How can I learn and practice prudence?
- Am I ready to do the unthinkable to see the unimaginable?
- In what ways am I willing to be a servant?
- Glory and honor come from God. Am I ready for the weight of it?

Chapter 16

NATURAL BORN SONS

ZION'S SONS

Now the Bereans were of more noble character than the Thessalonians, for they received the message with great eagerness and examined the Scriptures every day to see if what Paul said was true.

—Acts 17:11

IN BEREA, THE citizens were different. Was it because they had accepted a faulty bill of goods at times before this? Maybe deceivers with elegant words and persuasive logic had caused them great financial hardship or even loss of life. Everyone agreed that it would not happen again. Paul commended these Believers because they did not automatically accept all that Paul said. His fame was not sufficient nor his presentation so elegant as to convince them of the truth. To make sure that everything Paul said was true, each Berean eagerly and earnestly searched the Scriptures (the Old Testament—the New did not exist yet). Because of this quality in them, Paul said they were of *more noble character*, which literally meant of better birth. These who seek out the truth of God are a generation that can hold up their heads and not be swayed by the rhetoric of a person of prominence

In Psalm 133, excellence or noble birth is also found in the unity of the brothers. "How good and pleasant it is when brothers live together in unity! It is as if precious oil is poured on the head . . . falling on Mount Zion. For there the LORD bestows his blessing, even life forevermore."

Brotherly love is good for life forevermore. In the Hebrew one meaning of *blessing* is, "to cause to exist fully to us." This anointing envelops the whole group united together in their mindset as priests of God. How pleasant it is when brothers see eye to eye, with the same view. They are in a high-priestly position where they minister for and to God and not only to people of the same mindset.

Aaron, in Hebrew means, "teacher." Aaron was the minister between God and priest in the tabernacle. Aaron was set apart from the regular priests who served in a less intimate relationship to God. His position held a unity that was excellent, for it was in harmony with the Almighty. We too are priests unto God, and besides being priestly we are also kingly. We get excited about this because worldly training is to acquire power and fame. However, 1 Peter 2:9 describes the priestly position as God's idea of excellence. The KJV translation of the Bible reads, "But ye are a chosen generation, a royal priesthood, an holy nation, a peculiar people; that ye should shew forth the praises of him who hath called you out of darkness into his marvelous light." In *Young's*, it says it this way, "CHOSEN, literally, elect, (or choice, select, excellent) generation, a kingly priesthood, a hallowed nation, a people for an over (or thorough) making, that ye might tell forth the pleasing features of him who called you out of darkness with a view to His astonishing light." The excellent have a mandate to tell the pleasing features of God. Many "Christians" have failed to fulfill their job description, wanting only the title.

In John 15, Jesus commands us to love one another as Jesus loved us, and by doing so, we prove that we are His disciples. In the city of Zion, love is excellent because each loves the other over self. This love bears fruit that remains with us, pleasing our Heavenly Father. In doing the Father's business, Saints bear fruit within themselves and that they share it with others.

Proverbs 8:6 (KJV) says, "Hear: for I will speak of excellent things." In the Hebrew language "excellent" is the word *naw-gheed*, from a commander who occupies the front, either military or religious, such as an excellent thing, the chief, governor, noble prince, or ruler. It comes from a word in Hebrew that is a primary root meaning *to front*, that is, to stand boldly out opposite; by implication, to manifest; figuratively to announce always by word of mouth to one present to declare, and expound in speaking." From these descriptive words, we can see why we, the beloved, strive for excellence. It brings us into nobility, our proper position in the Kingdom of Heaven.

In Proverbs 17:27 (KJV), it says that understanding is of an excellent spirit. In the Hebrew, it is from an unused root meaning, "to be cold or excellent, or figuratively, quiet." Now this is interesting because we do not think of someone having an excellent spirit as being cold. To us, to be cold is unapproachable or unfeeling. However, here in God's realm, cold is excellent. Let me give an example of a time at a luncheon when several people were trying to figure out who would ride with whom back to the conference. One person in the group said, "I'll ride back with this person because they have such a quiet spirit." That person knew the other person was not hot-tempered or with an unruly character.

DECISIONS

Two kingdoms run throughout the Bible. To every person, one of these two dwelling places is their allotment because of the decisions they make. Let's start at Noah, who had three sons: Shem, Ham and Japheth (see Gen. 5:32; 1 Chron. 1:4). These three go into the world and produce the lineage to this present generation. Ham and Japheth's descendants end up in Shinar, where they thought so highly of themselves that they decided to build a tower up to God (see Gen. 11:1–9). This is the tower of Babel—Babylon—meaning *confusion*. The land of confusion is the kingdom of the enemy and of the people who live in a worldly manner. In addition, this spirit of confusion is the great whore on the beast depicted in Revelation 14:8–18:21.

Shem, in the Hebrew language means, *name, authority, and renown.* Shem will produce the lineage of the Hebrews. This is the ancestry of Jesus and those that know Him, Christians (see Eph. 2:5–13), those who are the *anointed ones* who are not of this world. It is these that form a chain of renown, a certainty of faith, and a confession of truth that is strong until the end. These are the Kingdom Believers, illustrated as candlesticks in the beginning of Revelation. They are present at the judgment and victory pronounced in chapter 18, and the lambs in Mount Zion, alongside Jesus. They are also the Bride later in Revelation.

Every human being comes from a birth, a nativity. The focus of a person's life is tied to the land where that person dwells. The choice of habitation a person makes holds the person's reward and brings them to account for how they lived. These people are of two types: the worldly and the godly.

There is a remnant that knows and understands what it means to be sons of God. Moreover, they understand God's visitation comes to all humankind, no matter our condition, heritage, or status. This visitation (judgment) is for eternity; depending on our decisions made here on earth. The land we have chosen for our heritage is the land the Lord will judge us for.

> In the place where you were created, in the land of your ancestry, I will judge you.
>
> —Ezekiel 21:30

There is a revealing of this land of ancestry found further on in Ezekiel 23 (see in KJV). In verse 16, those who have been taken in and easily persuaded are those who have gone after the world, doting on the things of the world and esteeming the ways and looks of humankind. Doting in *Hebrew,* "is the *native* power of breathing and blowing. It is applied to the *more violent affections of the mind,* especially love between the sexes." In verse 15 we read that the mind is alienated out of them. Here the word *alienated* tells us the reasons why their belief in God is torn off. It is because of *dyed attire:* these two words, dyed attire, are both reference #2871 in *Strong's,* which means, "headbands, tiaras, turbans," signifying that what is in their mind is of the world, materialistic, unjust, unrighteous, and impure. This love or doting that God's people had was really for worldly things, *after the manner of the Babylonians of Chaldea, the land of their nativity.* These who are alienated are the confused. Their birthplace is Babylon (Ezek. 23:15 KJV). The false believer is alienated from God. Here *alienated* is reference #3363 in *Strong's,* and partially means: "*to be torn off, to be torn away;* hence—(1) *to be dislocated,* as a limb. (2) metaph: *to be alienated* from any one (Ezek. 23:17)." Therefore, they continue to go the way of destruction. The next verse goes on to say that the mind of God was alienated from them (Ezek. 23:18–19 KJV). This alienated in verse 18 is reference #5361 in *Strong's* "(whence the future is formed), *to be torn from; metaph: to be alienated from* (Ezek. 23:18—as to be cleft or broken)." The thoughts of God are broken from them because of what they breathe after, chasing after the things on their heads (figuratively, turbans, etc.), meaning in their thoughts.

Christians, whose mindset is in the world, have broken from God's thinking. They have the opposite of what is on the heads of the priestly beloved of God who have headbands that say, HOLINESS TO THE LORD (Ex. 28:36). Ezekiel 16:3 (KJV) presents the location of these Christians. It says, ". . . thy nativity is of the land of Canaan . . . ." Canaan is the Promised Land, the land of Israel, Jerusalem, and Zion—the place that God has chosen for Himself and those that follow Him, making plain the verse that says that as a person thinks in his heart so is he, and that what land he lusts after, he will be judged in and for.

One of the requirements of any Believer is that they must be born from above. So how does that happen? The answer, *the Spirit is like the wind and it blows where it will* (see John 3:3–8). The Holy Spirit brings light to clean up the mess they have made out of their life. He brings Christians into the supernatural Light of the life of the Spirit who tirelessly moves Believers into the Kingdom of Heaven, where they are numbered as one born in Zion; the home country of the Sons of God.

Being born in a place, the individual has the ability to have their total heart, mouth, and mind speak the same, making our mindset native to that place. When Saints are born in Zion, the mind shares authority with Jesus for actions made evident in the natural.

Believers mature in the ways of Zion. This land defines the person— everything you dream of, everything known, is forming the person's characteristics that declare the pedigree where they originated.

Here in Ezekiel, the word, *born* in the Hebrew means, "to bear young or to show lineage." When reborn, we receive the birthright of Jesus—the second Adam and not the first Adam. We are born anew into the lineage of Jesus Christ (1 Cor.15:22, 45) to bring forth the Jesus generation.

Psalm 15 describes the citizens of Zion, the citizens who abide in the light, sojourning in Zion. They live in closeness to God's presence.

The Lord wants the flesh submitted totally to the Spirit (see Psa. 15:1–5). So the character and attitudes are of a person who walks in integrity, has a blameless life, walks uprightly, works righteousness with his heart, is cheerful, and behaves uprightly. He is one who speaks truth in his heart, does not slander, does no evil to a neighbor, does no reproach against a friend, and in whose eyes a reprobate is despised. He honors those who fear the Lord. He sees the Lord for who He is and swears to his own hurt and does not change. He is one who admits his sin. He does not put money out on interest nor does he take a bribe against the innocent. A person doing these things will never be moved from the Lord. Here is a road map, the goal in Kingdom life.

Stability comes from bonding to the Father's values and thoughts. Psalm 24:5–6 (NASB) says that they receive a blessing from the LORD and righteousness from the God of his salvation. This is the generation of those who seek Him, Who seek Your face. These can lift up their head, for they have done good. This is what Adonai said to Cain in Genesis 4:7. If you do good, lift up your head. However, Cain did not care. His eyes were on Abel, not on God, and Cain's thoughts became torn from his rightful birthplace.

The Best Dwelling Place

God has a love for Zion, choosing it as His dwelling place. There God is present. In Psalm 48:3 forward, it says that Zion is where God has made Himself known as a fortress. When kings advance, terror seizes them, and they are destroyed. Zion is secure forever. As we mediate on God's unfailing love, righteousness, and His judgments, Saints can view and count every tower in Zion. They can tell of its magnificence to the next generation. God guides the beloved to the end, as the name of the Lord is a strong tower. The name of Jesus towers above all else in this world. He is our great fortress against every attack. Our view from Him as our tower broadens our prospective and opens our eyes to victory.

Saints go up to Zion—not the highest mountain in the natural—but in the supernatural. None can compare to Zion. This is where God is *in our face* (He is present) far above the laws of the natural. We fly away with the Spirit, enabling contact with the supernatural and viewing things differently. This does not lift a person with pride or boasting, but we soar above the natural elements of life and have our Father's eyes. A person is lowered in humility while at the same time lifted, as we come closer to God, seeking God in such a way, the search persuades and invites us to view Him. Christians have the privilege to come alongside, setting us in high places with Jesus (see Eph. 2:6).

Wider and deeper views of the qualities Saints are to possess can be found in Psalm 101. David made a decision to have his mind set on certain things that he might not sin against the Lord. Jesus, as a son of David, also learned to have this view. The Lord has given the knowledge of the secret and ability to attain it, not only for David, but also for all of the beloved.

Here in parts of Psalm 101 (paraphrased), is a division of what the sons of God would do and would not do. "I will sing of your love and justice . . . . careful to lead a blameless life . . . I will walk in my house with a blameless heart . . . . set before my eyes no vile thing. The deeds of faithless men I hate; . . . Men of perverse heart shall be far from me; . . . nothing to do with evil. Whoever slanders his neighbor in secret, him will I put to silence; whoever has haughty eyes and a proud heart, him will I not endure. My eyes will be on the faithful in the land, . . . he whose walk is blameless will minister to me. No one who practices deceit will dwell in my house. No one who speaks falsely will stand in my presence. Every morning I will put to silence all the wicked in the land. I will cut off every evildoer from the city of the LORD."

In the revealing of David's life, his immediate household did not attain to God's high standards, but his aim was good. He targeted God's Kingdom. Jesus, from the lineage of David's house, accomplished and maintains these attributes. Thus, the psalm also portrays the household of Jesus and is to be our target. See how David says that doing these things will silence the wicked in the land and cut off the evildoer from the city. This action has a powerful force! If Saints will turn our desires to do what is done in Heaven, we can accomplish mighty things in the world. Setting our eyes on the goal, we learn what is required to live in Zion. We see that outside the Kingdom of Heaven, there are dogs and sorcerers and whoremongers and murderers and idolaters and whosoever loves and makes a lie (see Rev. 22:15 KJV). What we see with our natural eyes, Zion is here parallel in the supernatural.

Once we dwell in Zion, and the heavenly mindset is established in our life, our stand is cemented, and nothing shakes us. Nothing can come in and attack us, though going outside those who do evil and live in darkness assail us. Immature and unrecognized Saints live outside of Zion, abounding in the cares of the world and having no rest of God in themselves. They are immature, having failed to recognize the wisdom and understanding of the truth of the Living God. However, as Saints enter into more of the light, as they become pure in heart and live with clean hands, they settle down to attain and stay in Zion. Even as trials assail them, they keep their mind's eye on Jesus and look to Him as their stronghold.

When we have our dwelling place in Zion, we learn as a baby and we mature in that culture and establish a view of God's Kingdom. Here in Zion, Believers are developing keener senses. They see with different eyes. Their touch is more sensitive. Their taste and smell are more acute. They verge upon the supernatural and that affects the natural. We experience a taste of real life. What Christians learn growing up in Zion fills the rooms of our mind to capacity and does not allow room for any ideas outside that arena. Having the mind of Christ, Saints are to be comfortable there in the light of Zion. They are to be completely happy to live and settle down in permanent cohabitation. Letting a fire shine from our being, many of the lost see this natural phenomenon and watch the blaze—Jesus came to start a fire on the earth (see Luke 12:49)! We as the lamp, hold the living flame within us.

Psalm 87:6 says that the Lord shall count when He registers the peoples, "This one was born in Zion." To have God enroll you as being born in Zion is awesome. The God of Truth says, "I no longer call you a servant, but number you as being born in My house. Now you're a son of God." We have the legal rights to the lot or heritage of those born in the house of God. Jesus learned directly from the presence of His Father. This face-to-face lifestyle is very deep; deep alongside deep, not just deep calling to deep. It has *no space* in between: it is touching; having no gap, but a continuous rubbing with each other.

The nobles and princes with a more excellent character, who are born in Zion, are in the book of registry, written by the finger of God into the lineage of His family.

He has set his foundation at the base of the holy mountain that is set apart; the LORD loves the gates where Saints enter Zion, more than he loves all the dwellings of Jacob. Glorious and weighty things are said of you, O city of God: Selah . . . "This one was born in Zion in the light." Indeed, of Zion it will be said, "This one and that one were born in her, and the Most High himself will establish her." The LORD will write in the register of the peoples: "This one was born in Zion." Selah. As they make music they will sing, "All my fountains are in you" (see Psa. 87:1–7).

Many people will know God, but to those who know His secrets, know Him intimately, of them He says, "This one and that one were born in Zion." Zion-born people know and experience God as a friend, and that surpasses natural heritage. It surpasses the things of this world's system. To be a native of Zion is to understand the "Kingdom of Light," a place without darkness anywhere.

The Bride of Christ (women and men of Zion), are those who are doing what Jesus did. They are evangelists, winning souls and doing incredible things as they store up treasures in Heaven! They praise God as He purifies them into holy and mature sons of God.

With a birth certificate designed in Zion and engraved by the hand of God, there is nothing impossible for we that believe. Our light is no longer hidden, but it is set in public on a stand, where the blaze forces darkness back. The righteous shout, "Come out of her, My people," and "Come, Lord Jesus, come," on our lips. As we witness the mighty acts of the God of Wonder, He glories in His people. Humble and contrite of heart, Saints bow before God who lifts us up into heavenly places where

Jesus is known and Paul is recognized. Followers are known as the sons of God. Because Jesus backs us, evil will be defeated by the Host of Heaven.

Citizens of Zion have the foundations of the apostles and prophets, men of renown—world changers as the Holy Spirit flowed through them. We have the history of the fiery remnant of the heroes of God who did exploits—reminders that encourage and strengthen us to continue in our daily living for Him. We are the Bride of Jesus, who is the King of Glory, and the Lord of the Host of Heaven (see Psa. 24:10).

> Consequently, you are no longer foreigners and aliens, but fellow citizens with God's people and members of God's household, built on the foundation of the apostles and prophets, with Christ Jesus himself as the chief cornerstone. In him the whole building is joined together and rises to become a holy temple in the Lord. And in him you too are being built together to become a dwelling in which God lives by his Spirit.
> —Ephesians 2:19–22

- In what ways can I prove logical and elegant words are true or false?
- How do I become a person with a more excellent spirit?
- There are two dwelling places. As a son of God, how do I live in Zion?
- What have I been telling of the pleasing features of God?

Chapter 17

THE COURAGEOUS MIND

Small is the gate and narrow is the road that leads to life, and only a few find it.

—Matthew 7:14; see also Luke 13:24

THERE IS A way that seems right to humankind, and it is the wide gate and path that leads to destruction. But the small gate and narrow way is the way the courageous travel, and few are they who find it (see Matt. 7:13–14). For Saints to live the life of the Kingdom of God, it takes discipline, training, trust, and looking to the Eternal God for all truth. The courageous go on past the elemental teachings. They go for the meatier content of the Word and experience with Jesus. They travel the narrow way entering into the Kingdom, and they enter like wrestlers! They are bold in action and seize the moment. They are the recognized in the supernatural realm and in the world—obedient only to the One True God.

The valiant of God see that far country and carry the treasures of that land to the needy people here, to supply what is lacking in the life of the poor or to those in dire want. They are different, and viewed from afar, they are like Elijah. No one wants to mess with them. They call things down from Heaven and go where few will tread. They travel the narrow way of faith, and hope beyond hope in what God has promised, as they stay on the path of righteousness, for they know their Beloved, they are His and He is theirs (see Song of Solomon 2:16).

It is a fight to stay in the narrow way of truth. In fact, Paul says we are to contend for the faith, and *Young's* exhorts us to agonize openly for the faith (see Jude v. 3, NASB). We are to take hold of the eternal life to which we are called (see 1 Tim. 6:12 NASB). To reach our goal and win the race, it is done as a wrestler. We present the life in the Kingdom of Heaven as an argument in the ongoing war for souls, struggling earnestly to overrule the thoughts of others in the kingdom of this world. We overcome every stronghold by the name of Jesus, by what His blood accomplished, and by dying to our self-life as we confess that He is Lord.

In striving with unseen forces, we fight against an adversary who would love to keep us in darkness and marginalized to the max. The first bouts of fighting go on in our own lives. From there, the arena extends to other venues. No matter the scope of the territory, we are more than conquerors through Jesus who loves us.

Sometimes, God speaks plainly, but we hear the first part and forget the part we need to do. We need to trust Him and do all He has asked us to do. We struggle to be like Jesus. Sometimes, we think it is too difficult. Why even try? But, as Peter said, "Where would we go, Lord? You have the words of life." God has given grace and mercy and it is His good pleasure to give us the Kingdom. He has given us the power to become sons of God. Therefore, the thought of being defeated cannot overcome us as we push on toward the goal of becoming like Jesus. The natural and spiritual world recognize that we have been with Jesus. We have acquired the precious oil and broken the enslaving yoke of sin.

It is not in how well we sound in our presentation that persuades God to act in the affairs of humankind. Jesus is the power of the Kingdom of Heaven. We share authority with Him as we allow Him to move through us as vessels. As we step out in faith, the anointing of Jesus brings forth the manifestations of God. The enormity of the Kingdom of Heaven is beyond a Christian's capacity to understand. We are awed as our knowledge and understanding increase and we know more of the depth, height, breadth, and length of God's Kingdom. Even if the fear of failing impedes our way, we eagerly trust what God can and will do for His name's sake. We witness signs and wonders, for Jesus said, "I tell you the truth, anyone who has faith in me will do what I have been doing. He will do even greater things than these" (see John 14:12). Greater things! This is amazing. Come on, we can do this because He said we can! Let your imagination go. Sail away in the Spirit and see the wonders of God. Be united in one mind with Christ and do not waver in doubt (see Heb. 10:23; Jas. 1:6). Christians are required to prepare themselves by the girding up of their loins with God's justice and serving Him in right acts.

God's way is a narrow way, and we find that it takes exertion on our part to find and follow it. Luke 13:24, in *Young's* says, "STRIVE, literally agonize (i.e. be as energetic as *wrestlers* are) to go in through the [narrow door; for many, I tell you] shall seek (or desire, in a general way), to go in, and shall not have strength (of mind necessary to make the attempt)."

Strength of mind is a key element and one of strong passion and emotion. It is a violent force, a mindset that dares to believe, to hope, to love, and to contend for the faith. It is hard to keep our mind from believing what we see in front of us. It takes strength to stay the course and focus our attention on the hope of things not yet seen.

When the disciples could not cast a demon out of a person, Jesus was indignant, and said, "How long will I be with you?" How upsetting it must have been for Him to be teaching daily, demonstrating authority and power to them, and they still didn't get it. They were still lacking in trust, not having the strength of mind to grasp what and whom they were experiencing. "Strength of mind" is an unfamiliar phrase because physical strength, knowledge, and wealth are what humankind considers powerful (see Jer. 9:23). Strength of mind is what Jesus tells the disciples they need, as do we. It is essential for Believers to tenaciously keep their mindset on the way the supernatural world works instead of how the natural world works. We battle not against flesh and blood but rulers of evil forces in heavenly realms (see Eph. 6:12). Jesus is serious about the Kingdom of God being lived out here on earth. We need to be serious about the things Jesus is serious about!

God has always said that He moves in the affairs of humankind for His name's sake—not ours. He wants to be known here on earth through us, by the renown of the name "Jesus." The spiritual kingdom recognized who Paul was because of his relationship with Jesus and because of his trust in God. Bold Christians are not stagnating in word or deed as long as they breathe and live for Jesus. In Acts 4:17–20, Peter and John were commanded and threatened to stop speaking in the name of Jesus, but they answered that they could not but be witnesses to what they knew. The act of declaring something is to make known what you know. We are to make known God's renown, His measure, and His weightiness in this age.

Action is required to reach the lost. There are millions of walking dead people out there needing to hear the salvation message to live! In Proverbs 11:30, it says that to *win souls is wise*. Jesus commanded Christians to go preach the good news, declaring freedom and release to captives. Jesus did not say that we needed to be evangelists. In fact, only Philip was called to the office of evangelist, but every one of the

Apostles went from their homes telling everyone about the gospel. Today, Christians must not dare do less. Here in the Western world we have been duped into thinking we only need to do what we are *gifted* or *called* to do. Humbug! That is man's thinking. Jesus said, *"GO! Preach the gospel to every creature"* (see Matt. 24:14; 26:13; Mark 16:15; Luke 9:6; 1 Pet. 4:6, 17; Rev. 14:6). Tell it, don't be ashamed of the gospel of Christ (see Rom. 1:16). If Christians do not tell others about Jesus, He will be ashamed of us and not speak to His Father on our behalf. If Jesus is not speaking on our behalf, exploits will be missing from our life. One of the meanings of blessed is, *well spoken of.*

God even uses people who do not know Him to complete His plans. God will bring about His expected end by whomever obeys. We can choose obedience or rebellion. However, God has appointed us to greatness. He has given us work to do, as stated so many times in the Old and New Testaments. We are to win the world by bringing good news to people who are utterly dying. Like Jesus, we are to destroy the works of the devil. Jesus came that we might be free and have life—abundant life. Those things loosed in Heaven are available in our present. Freedom has not been closed off. By the life we live, we display the Kingdom of Heaven. With the counsel of God, the exploits of Heaven will amaze us here on earth.

THE REMNANT

Those who become the warriors, the valiant, and the heroes are those who have stood throughout time even though they sometimes knew failure. However, they pressed on and dared to bravely speak and live out of this world's regime. They lived on the cutting edge. Uncommon, they contended as wrestlers for the trust they have in God. They never gave up. They knew that what we bind on earth will be bound in Heaven, and what we loose here on the earth will be loosed there (see Matt. 16:19).

The courageous of mind are happily content, they are fearless, eager to go into the adventure—like a child wanting to experience everything. A good full mind is strong in the Lord. Heroes are neither weary nor faint in their mind (see Heb. 12:3). Weary in their flesh at times, they continually encourage themselves in the Lord. They do have battles, and some are great against them. Nevertheless, they stand unyielding in the truth.

These mighty ones do not blend into the crowd—but like an obelisk, they stand out, not because of their stature, but because of the integrity of their character. If people gather around them because of fame, two things happen: either the valiant of Jesus train their followers to live undaunted by the world and the followers become courageous, or the followers soon drop away, not wanting to get that close—that radical—that far out—in fact out of their minds! And gladly, the bold agree that they are out of their own mind, they have the mind of Christ. They have decided to go all the way, possessed by the Holy Spirit. They will give it all and let go of the world. These "sons of God," have joined covenant with Jesus, slaying giants who have no covenant with God!

They know that if they *live or die they do so in Christ* (see Rom. 14:8). Their eyes see their homeland where people are whole. They understand that here people need love, and they give compassion to those who need to be touched, healed, refreshed, and released from bondage. Wounds are anointed and bandaged. The poor, the widow, and the orphan are cared for and given a voice, where all acquire justice and righteousness.

The whole world points at these inspiring giants and exclaims, "Look, those who turn the world upside down have come here!" Upside down? No, in God's eyes, they've turned it right side up. The courageous abandon all the world offers in order to do the impossible. With strength of mind they do things they have never seen before—walking on water, bullets dropping, or guns not firing. They have learned to laugh at death. Undaunted, they give their lives for the gospel; for they understand that it is the power of God to salvation (see 1 Cor. 1:18; Rom. 1:16). As they endure hardships, imprisonment, mocking, and beating, they share in the suffering of Christ, and they join in His Glory (see 1 Pet. 4:12–13).

They do great exploits like some of the first events in the past: the first rapture when Enoch walked with God right into Heaven; when Noah preached repentance for one hundred years while building something no one had ever seen for an event never heard of! Moreover, in doing so, he condemns the world. The world spoke one language until another first at Babel, when God's visit confuses the words of the human race, and diversity in language comes to planet Earth. Abraham goes to a land he's never seen, believes God, and becomes the first person with a new identify as the father, not of a nation, but nations. Abraham sees what happens to the faithless when God visits and when fire and sulfur fall from the sky without the aid of planes or bombs. He and Sarah are the first to birth a child conceived through supernatural intervention by God.

After he encounters the first tree unconsumed by fire, Moses confronts the god of the earth (pharaoh) whom he persuades to submit to the Almighty God with signs and wonders. Moses is the first to deliver an enslaved nation. He builds the first tabernacle as a place to meet with God. In the natural, Joshua brings a new generation into a new land, carrying Joseph's bones and the Ten Commandments of God into a land unknown to them.

Joseph's name means, "he adds," and, "the Law defines sin." Think about the meaning of the name Joseph and the Law. It reveals a truth of future promise. In that (the bones), or the strength of He who adds grace and mercy to the Law crossed the river into the Promised Land, giving more meaning to what Paul said about still keeping the Law, and that the Spirit of the Law is nestled in mercy and grace.

The wonders of the heavenly Kingdom continue as the bones of a prophet, Elisha, raise a man from the dead! Food and water are supernaturally supplied. A virgin conceives supernaturally from the Holy Spirit and births the Holy Son of God, Jesus; He walks on water, expels demons, cleanses lepers, and is the first to open the eyes and ears of those born blind and deaf—all "firsts" that mark Jesus as the One who is to come (Matt. 11:4–6). Jesus lives and then dies on an execution stake. He is the first to descend into hell and take the keys of death and hell from the enemy and rise to life again! Jesus has all authority and power. He is the leader of the army of Heaven, and He lives forevermore sitting at the right hand of the Father. The exploits of God's people continue down through the ages, even to this age.

All these were people of little renown until they chose to accept God's invitation to join His plan for their life and embrace the real to leave the artificial in the world. They bravely moved forward in faith as the remarkable journey began.

Go from Here

In John 14:31 (NASB), it says, "Get up, let us go from here." And if you read on, no one physically travels anywhere. This *going* is in the mind. In the Greek language, it is "to awake, rouse self—from what was previously done or said." It is to move onward to improved things that are new to us, but of which we are capable by our renewed nature. This also is what happens to Philip (see Acts 8:26), when told by the Spirit to arise and go down the road where he meets the Ethiopian eunuch. In the Greek the meaning of arise is to *rouse yourself*.

In John 15:4–11 (paraphrased), Jesus teaches about abiding in the Kingdom where Saints live from Jesus' point of view, in the supernatural, past the nominal Christian's life, abiding in the lifted up place of Zion.

They have the proof of being disciples, *ones who are taught* by Jesus. Jesus encourages, edifies, and gives them knowledge of what is to come. The scene continues into the place of "ifs." He tells them, *If* you do what I command you—love each other. *If* the world hates you—it hated me first. *If* you belonged to the world, it would love you. *If* they persecuted me, they will persecute you also. *If* they obey My teaching, they will obey yours also (because we say only what Jesus says). They will treat you this way because of My name. Then Jesus continues and condemns the world because of humankind's sin. In verse 22 he says, "*if* I had not come and spoken to them, *if* I had not done among them what no one else did, . . . "Yet they have hated both Me and My Father." This is an awesome depiction of the mirror reflection of a supernatural Saint. It is a way to understand if faith is in us (see 2 Cor. 13:5). Those Saints are known outside the regular congregation as the remnant, with their mindset placed on the certainty of the Words of God. Their actions are unprecedented and supernatural things happen.

There are valiant Believers out there with first events, even if we have not heard of them. Heroes do not look at the numbers; instead, they see the God of the innumerable. Of course, we can think we are all alone. Just as Elijah cried out to God that he was the only one left, God said that was not so, there were seven thousand left who had not bowed the knee to Baal and whose mouths have not kissed him (see 1 Kings 19:14–18). Elijah did not see those seven thousand, but God did. Do not worry about who else is in the battle, only be steadfast in obedience and faithfulness (see Rev. 13:10; 14:12).

Confident hope springs eternal in the souls of the valiant as they wait in expectancy of every promise. Jesus died that there would always be enough and more than enough for all Believers (see Rom. 5:17).

There is a rest that Heaven supplies. This godly *rest* matures in a Believer's life as he has the *strength of mind* to allow what the Word of God has developed. It cost our lives, as Saints become laid-down lovers. We must turn from our own ideas and make room in our mind's imagination for the stretching and filling of the possibilities from the great *I AM*. He who created the universe, hung the stars in place and named them all. Yet He was willing to give all that we might be heroes and possess the Kingdom of Heaven right now! Jesus is who He says He is. A powerful pastor from Africa advises Americans not to be too tame. He encourages them to be adventurous and invade people's space and act like Jesus.

Heroes of God have the business of the Kingdom of Heaven to do, for Jesus left the taking of the kingdom of this world to people like you and me. We have a responsibility to become nobility, becoming more committed and determined than ever before. I am striving for these things too. God is amazing. He has chosen Saints to make God visible on the earth.

There are certain things that seem to bring miracles. If you look at all God's people of renown, they cherish fellowship with Jesus and are intently about the Father's business, pleading repentance and winning souls so that the house of God would be full. They carry the Kingdom of Heaven here on earth! They got it—that we Believers carry the Kingdom of Heaven to everyone wherever we go. We have the Kingdom of God here, right now in this time.

Not only do demons of violence bow, but nature also bows as in the violent storm in Matthew 8:24–26. Everything must bow its knee at the renown of Jesus (see Phil. 2:10). Others have had remarkable things happen as they dedicated themselves to God. Reese Howell, with others, prayed for Britain's safety during the war, and God delivered Britain by providing fog so heavy that the enemy's planes and ships could not come near land. In Indonesia during a revival, preachers going from village to village walked on water. There are others like Henry Gruver who believed the God of Heaven and Earth, and changed the course of the natural elements, diverting a storm from demolishing their vegetable garden. He also "prayer walks" the earth and redeems areas that have been devastated by the crimes of humankind where the blood cries out from the ground and vegetation no longer grows. But after redeeming the area with cleansing prayer, the water once again returns, and the grass grows. Jesus came to redeem the whole earth. Yes, God will move nature for us! God has set boundaries in nature, but He will move them if need be, for those that love and trust Him.

On one of the first occasions when God moved nature, Moses raised his hands to part the Red Sea. The sea saw it and fled! Elisha asked God to open the eyes of his servant that he might see the hills full of horses and chariots of fire all around. David raised his hands and asked that God would accept this act as the representation of the evening sacrifice. Jesus turns water into wine, and rocks will praise Jesus if people do not. If you have faith for it, God even has the natural elements take notice and obey! Where are the shining faces, those that see through the supernatural veil, and those warring with their hands?

Many miracles happen in other nations. Saints have driven through raging rivers and walked over snow-covered mountain in bare feet to take the good news to others. People like Richard Wurmbrand, founder of the Voice of the Martyrs, was released after being tortured fourteen years for Christ. Food is multiplied, healings of every kind occur, AIDS hospitals are cleared out, people are translated, angels are seen, and storms obey. Terrorists lay down their guns for Jesus; drug lords leave their addiction and business for Jesus; and the poor have what they need. The *Shekinah* glory covers towns. Men kneel in the street as they feel the awesome presence of God. There are reports of gold teeth coming into people's mouths. I have seen Believers skin and clothes sprinkled with gold—dustings of gold appears on them, or drop from nothing—from mid-air as it floats down.

Saints such as Keith Wheeler, who carries the cross around the world, Jackie Pullinger of St. Stephens Ministry who evangelized a drug-infested part of Hong Kong called the Walled City. These are only a few heroes here mentioned, but all see a better country. They know to whom they belong. They are living examples for us. It's time for the church to arise—to wake! We must put off our slumber and go out to meet the Groom! He is in the streets, in the marketplace where the merchandizing of the human race takes place right before our eyes.

> Far better it is to dare mighty things, to win glorious triumphs even though checkered by failure, than to take rank with those poor spirits who neither enjoy much nor suffer much because they live in the gray twilight that knows neither victory or defeat.
>
> —Theodore Roosevelt.

CONTACT INFORMATION

To order additional copies of this book, please visit
www.redemption-press.com.
Also available on Amazon.com and BarnesandNoble.com
Or by calling toll free 1 (888) 305-2967.

CPSIA information can be obtained at www.ICGtesting.com
Printed in the USA
BVOW05s1259010614

355052BV00001B/107/P